THE USBORNE
HISTORY OF BRITAIN
KINGS & QUEENS

Designed by Stephen Moncrieff,
Samantha Barrett, Tom Lalonde & Steve Wood

Edited by Jane Chisholm
Consultant: Dr. Anne Millard

Previous page: The marriage of James I
of Scotland to Joan Beaufort

Below: Edward VI's coronation procession
through the streets of London, 1547

THE USBORNE
HISTORY OF BRITAIN
KINGS & QUEENS

Ruth Brocklehurst,
Emily Bone, Kate Davies,
Hazel Maskell & James Maclaine

Illustrated by Ian McNee

Usborne Quicklinks

The Usborne Quicklinks Website is packed with thousands of links to all the best websites on the internet. The websites include information, video clips, sounds, games and animations that support and enhance the information in Usborne internet-linked books.

To visit the recommended websites for this book, go to the Usborne Quicklinks Website at **www.usborne.com/quicklinks** and enter the keywords **Kings and Queens**.

When using the internet please follow the internet safety guidelines displayed on the Usborne Quicklinks Website. The recommended websites in Usborne Quicklinks are regularly reviewed and updated, but Usborne Publishing Ltd. is not responsible for the content or availability of any website other than its own. We recommend that children are supervised while using the internet.

CONTENTS

MONARCHY

This book tells the stories of the kings and
queens who have ruled in Britain through
the ages. Among them are brave warriors,
illustrious patrons, ruthless tyrants, fools,
saints and sinners. Some of their reigns
have been long and peaceful and some have
come to a sudden, sticky end. Together,
their lives form the thread that ties together
the events of Britain's past.

Henry IV, dressed in black, uses his
sword to cut his cousin, Richard II,
from a tangled-looking royal family tree.

Ruling Britannia

This timeline shows the different groups that ruled in parts of Britain before 1066, and the reigns of some of the most important early kings.

around 2,000 years ago

Britain is made up of several tribes, each led by a warrior chief.

43-410

Romans invade and conquer most of Britain, except for the Scottish tribes, who they refer to as Picts.

by 670

Seven Anglo-Saxon kingdoms — Northumbria, Mercia, East Anglia, Kent, Essex, Sussex and Wessex — have taken root in England.

around 500

An Irish tribe, called the Scots, invades Pictish territory in the west of Scotland.

from 450

Anglo-Saxon raiders attack and begin to settle in the south and east of Britain.

789

Vikings launch their first raids on Britain.

802-839
EGBERT

King of Wessex. Conquers Mercia around 825.

842-858
KENNETH MacAlpin

Unites Picts and Scots under his rule.

844-878
RHODRI 'Mawr'

Rules most of Wales by 872.

878

England is divided between the Anglo-Saxon kingdoms in the south and Viking territory, called the Danelaw, in the north.

871-899
ALFRED 'the Great'

King of Wessex. Egbert's grandson.

by 870

Vikings occupy the north and east of England, and parts of Scotland and Ireland.

959-975
EDGAR

The first king to be crowned following the ceremony that's still used by modern British monarchs.

1002-1014
BRIAN BORU

Overthrows the other kings in Ireland to become High King.

1003-1004

Swein 'Forkbeard', King of Denmark, invades England and declares himself King. This leads to a struggle for the throne between the Danes and Edgar's successors.

1042-1066
EDWARD 'the Confessor'

Dies without an heir, leaving England to face another war over who will be King.

THE
RISE OF THE KINGS

Britain hasn't always been a unified country with a single monarch, as it is today. Two thousand years ago, in the 1st century, the land was divided between more than 30 tribes. Each tribe was led by a warrior chief, but there weren't any kings and queens yet.

Then, after a series of wars and invasions, the first kings rose to power and the British nations began to take shape.

WARRIORS AND INVADERS

Two thousand years ago, the British tribes didn't think of themselves as belonging to one nation and they certainly didn't all look up to one ruler. Then, in the year 43, the Romans invaded and changed all that.

Rebel 'queen'

The British tribes didn't all accept Roman rule without a fight. Boudicca was a tribal leader who led a massive rebellion against the Romans in the year 60.

Legends say that when the Romans defeated her, she and her daughters poisoned themselves to avoid being captured.

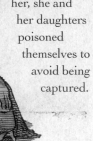

Roman rule

The Romans, who came from Rome, in Italy, had already conquered much of Europe. Over the next 50 years or so, they took control of most of Britain too. Only the Picts – who lived in what would later become Scotland – remained unconquered.

As part of the Roman Empire, Britain wasn't ruled by a king, but by an emperor who was usually based in Rome. Hundreds of Roman soldiers were stationed in Britain to enforce the Emperor's laws, and to protect the land against invasion.

Saxon raiders

In 410, the Romans left Britain to deal with invasions elsewhere in the Empire. The Britons were left alone to fight off a new wave of raiders – known as Angles, Saxons and Jutes – from what is now northern Germany and Denmark. From the year 450, the raiders began to settle in the south and east of England. Some came peacefully, but others took the land by force.

This is a marble bust of Roman Emperor Hadrian, who visited Britain in the year 122. He ordered a wall to be built to mark the Roman frontier. Hadrian's Wall still roughly marks part of the border between England and Scotland today.

This 13th-century painting shows the legendary King Arthur and his knights fighting off the Saxon invaders.

His story may not be true, but it has inspired writers, artists, and even kings ever since.

Henry VII even claimed to be descended from Arthur.

From warlords to kings

Legends written about the time of the invasions describe a Romano-British warrior named Arthur, who led local resistance to the Saxons. No one knows exactly what happened, but while some Britons did put up a fight, they failed to stop the invading forces from occupying the land.

The newcomers became known as Anglo-Saxons. They set up their own territories ruled by warlords, who started, boastfully, to call themselves kings.

Celts, Picts and Scots

In what is now Scotland, Picts and native Britons, who spoke Celtic languages, stayed in control. Then, around the year 500, an Irish tribe invaded the West Highlands and set up their own kingdom of Dalriada (see map on page 13). They were called the Scots, and it is from them that Scotland eventually took its name.

King's English

In the 5th century, most Britons spoke different variations of Celtic languages, and some also knew Latin, the Romans' language.

The Anglo-Saxons brought with them their own Germanic language. It gradually spread and developed to become the English language.

The word 'king' comes from the Anglo-Saxon *cyning*, which means leader of people, from *cynn*, or kin, meaning race or family.

HIGH KINGS AND VIKINGS

During the 5th and 6th centuries, the first Anglo-Saxon kings set up their own small kingdoms. A king lived off food and goods provided by the peasants who lived on his land. If he needed more of anything, he would lead his army to seize land or loot from rival kings. To keep his warriors loyal, he divided some of the spoils between them.

But it was a dangerous job being king. Many died in battle, or at the hands of followers who thought they'd do a better job themselves.

Kingly treasures

In 1939, archaeologists unearthed the grave of an Anglo-Saxon king at Sutton Hoo, in Suffolk.

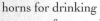

He was buried in a ship with lots of his belongings around him. These included a helmet (a replica is shown above), sword and shield, bowls, cups, horns for drinking from, and a type of harp known as a lyre.

Experts think the king was probably Redwald of East Anglia, who died around the year 625.

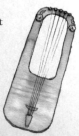

Gaining strength

Sometimes, a particularly powerful king would declare himself 'High King' over the others. This meant that weaker kings were supposed to swear loyalty to him as their overlord and give him land, goods or soldiers.

Gradually, the strongest kings built up their territories, and by the 7th century, there were seven main Anglo-Saxon kingdoms – Wessex, Essex, Kent, East Anglia, Mercia and Northumbria.

Higher powers

The first Anglo-Saxon settlers were pagans, who prayed to many gods. But, by the end of the 7th century, most Anglo-Saxons had converted to Christianity, guided by the teachings of the Pope in Rome.

Their ideas about kingship changed too. Now, kings weren't only warrior chiefs; they were also expected to be wise, just rulers whose royal birth set them above ordinary people.

Viking terror

The 8th century was a time of relative peace for the Anglo-Saxon kings. But that was all shattered when Britain came under a new and terrifying threat: boatloads of Scandinavian warriors, or Vikings, began to attack. In 789, they launched the first of many smash-and-grab raids on coastal settlements, churches and monasteries.

Then, in 865 a vast army of Danish Vikings invaded. This time, they planned to conquer Britain and stay for good.

Britain in the 8th and 9th centuries

- Pictish kingdoms
- Celtic kingdoms
- Anglo-Saxon kingdoms

Viking attacks:
- → Danes (from Denmark)
- → Norse (from Norway and Sweden)

The main British kingdoms are shown in capital letters on this map.

Orkney Islands

Western Isles

ATLANTIC OCEAN

PICTLAND

Dunkeld
Scone

Iona

DALRIADA

Dunadd

Edinburgh

Lindisfarne

NORTH SEA

STRATHCLYDE

NORTHUMBRIA

Hadrian's Wall

ULSTER

CONNAUGHT

Isle of Man

IRISH SEA

York

MIDE
Dublin

LEINSTER

GWYNEDD Chester

Offa's Dyke

MUNSTER

POWYS

MERCIA

EAST ANGLIA
Sutton Hoo

DYFED

GWENT

ESSEX

Cardiff

WESSEX
Winchester

London

KENT Canterbury

DUMNONIA

SUSSEX

ALFRED
'the Great'
871-899

Born: Wantage,
Oxfordshire c.849

Crowned: 871, possibly at
Kingston-on-Thames

Died: October 26, 899

Buried: Winchester

The first King of
the English and the only one
ever to be given the title,
'the Great'.

THE FIRST GREAT KING

By 870, the marauding Danes had conquered Northumbria, East Anglia and much of Mercia. Now they set their sights on Wessex. The Anglo-Saxons needed to put aside their differences to fight off the Vikings, but it would take a great leader to unite them. That man was Alfred.

Humble beginnings

As the fifth son of the King of Wessex, no one could have imagined that Alfred would grow up to become a great leader. He was a shy, devout child, who went with his father on two trips to Rome to meet the Pope, the head of the Christian Church.

Alfred loved listening to poems about heroic warriors. Growing up in a land under attack, he soon learned to become one himself.

Fighting for survival

Alfred became King of Wessex in 871. By then, he had already fought many battles against the Vikings. For a time, he paid them to stay away. But, early in 878, the Danes launched a massive attack.

The King fled to marshland in the south-west, but he wouldn't be beaten. He saw the pagan Vikings, who smashed monasteries and torched their precious libraries, as barbarians. This wasn't just a fight to save Wessex. It was a battle for civilization.

Alfred draws the line

By May, Alfred had amassed a huge army, and was ready to fight back. He overwhelmed the Vikings at the Battle of Edington, and they soon surrendered. But Alfred couldn't drive them out completely. So he set a line, from London to Chester, with his territory to the west and theirs – the 'Danelaw' – to the east.

King of the English

The war won, Alfred set about improving his kingdom. To strengthen it against future attacks, he reorganized the army, built up a navy and constructed a chain of fortified towns, known as 'burhs'.

Like most Anglo-Saxons, Alfred had grown up without being taught to read and write. He made up for this by learning Latin when he was 38, and setting up schools. He had many important texts translated into Anglo-Saxon, and even translated some himself.

Alfred's greatest achievement was to convince the Anglo-Saxons that they didn't belong to different tribes any more. They were all *Angelcynn* – the English. By 890, Alfred was no longer called King of Wessex, he was 'King of all the English'. But he's better known as Alfred the Great.

This gold and enamel jewel is known as the Alfred Jewel. It probably formed the head of a pointer stick, used for following words on a page while reading.

Around the edge is an Anglo-Saxon inscription, AELFRED MEC HEHT GEWYRCAN – "Alfred had me made."

Not great with cakes

A legend tells of how Alfred met a peasant woman while he was hiding in the marshes.

She left him to watch some cakes she was cooking, but Alfred was distracted and let them burn. Not knowing who he was, the woman scolded him.

It was then that her husband recognized the King. Fearing they'd be punished, they begged for mercy, but Alfred simply apologized.

EDWARD 'the Elder'
899-924

Accepted as overlord by the
other British kings.

AELFWEARD
924

Edward's son. Ruled for 15 days.

ATHELSTAN
924-39

Edward's son. The first king to
rule over all of England.

EDMUND I
939-946

Edward's son. Stabbed to death
during a feast.

EDRED
946-55

Edmund's brother. Drove the
Vikings out of York.

EDWIG
955-59

Edmund's son. Died, aged 19,
from an unknown illness.

EDGAR 'the Peaceful'
959-75

Edwig's brother.
Crowned twice in 973.

UNITING THE KINGDOM

In 899, Alfred died. In the wrong hands, all his work could have been undone. But, luckily, many of his successors were almost as great as he was.

Alfred's son, Edward the Elder, was a bold military leader. With the help of his sister Ethelfleda Queen of Mercia, he expanded his territory to take in Mercia and East Anglia. By 923, he was so powerful that most other British kings accepted him as their overlord.

Bloody battles

In 937, the Viking King of Dublin joined forces with other British kings and invaded England. At the Battle of Brunanburh, they faced the army of Alfred's grandson, King Athelstan. Hundreds were slain on both sides, but the English won in the end. Athelstan took over the Danelaw and became the first king to rule over the whole of England.

But the Vikings soon came back for more, and it wasn't until 954 that they were defeated altogether.

Peace and power

In 959, Alfred's great-grandson, Edgar, became King of a united England, and he made sure it stayed that way. He brought in standard laws and currency throughout the land, and he kept peace with his Danish subjects in the north by involving them in local government.

Under Edgar, England was better organized, wealthier and stronger than ever – and he wanted to celebrate his achievements. So, in 973, he staged two spectacular coronations at Bath and Chester.

Edgar's crowning glory

To make a really big impression, Dunstan, Archbishop of Canterbury, set out a new form of coronation ceremony for King Edgar. It is still followed, more or less, by modern British kings and queens. Here's the order of ceremony:

1. The oath: Edgar promised to protect his people and the Church, and uphold the laws of the land.

2. Anointing: the Archbishop blessed the King with holy oil.

This picture of Edgar was made in 966.

3. Crowning: the King was handed the crown jewels and the crown was placed on his head.

4. Homage: Edgar's leading subjects lined up before him and paid homage (swore loyalty) to him, one by one.

At Chester, as many as eight other British kings paid homage to Edgar. Then, they were said to have rowed him along the River Dee as a symbol of their promise to serve him, "by sea and by land".

RHODRI

'Mawr' ('the Great')

844–878

King of Gwynedd, later ruled all of
Wales, except Dyfed and Gwent.

Died in battle against
Alfred the Great.

HYWEL

'Dda' ('the Good')

c.904–950

Rhodri Mawr's grandson

King of Deheubarth, then King
of all Wales by 942.

Reformed the Welsh
legal system.

Offa's Dyke has worn down
over the centuries, but its
remains still cut a swathe
through the landscape.

RULING WALES

While England was becoming a united kingdom, Wales looked set to do the same. The Welsh had only been partially conquered by the Romans, and resisted the Anglo-Saxons, too. As a result, from the 5th century, the Welsh language and a distinct Welsh culture developed.

A patchwork of small kingdoms grew out of the Celtic tribes that had existed before Roman rule. The stronger kings expanded their territories. By the 8th century, a handful of larger kingdoms was in charge.

Setting the limit

One of the most important kings to shape early Wales was an Anglo-Saxon, Offa of Mercia. In the 780s, he ordered a vast defensive earthwork to be built along the boundary between his lands and the Welsh kingdom of Powys. Offa's Dyke, as it is known, still roughly marks the border between England and Wales today.

Welsh unity

Although there were frequent skirmishes along the border, behind Offa's Dyke the Welsh kingdoms grew stronger, especially during the reigns of two particularly powerful kings: Rhodri Mawr and Hywel Dda.

Rhodri became King of Gwynedd in 844. Through marriage, inheritance and possibly conquest, he brought together most of Wales under his rule. A great warrior king, he beat off attacks from the Vikings in the west and the English in the east.

Wales couldn't stay united for long. According to Welsh custom, a king's land had to be divided between all his sons. So, when Rhodri died, his kingdom was broken up.

Laying down the law

At the start of the 10th century, Rhodri's grandson, Hywel, inherited a small kingdom in the west of Wales. Like his grandfather, he expanded his territories and took the title 'King of all Wales'. Unlike him, Hywel avoided war with the English king by accepting him as his overlord.

But Hywel's greatest achievement was to bring all of Wales under one set of laws for the first time. The laws were written in Welsh and included some rights for women, at a time when most laws were written in Latin and women were usually seen as the property of their fathers or husbands.

Hywel's laws remained in force until the 16th century. But, despite the successes of a few great leaders, the Welsh were never permanently united, and were never fully independent from England.

Wolves at the gate?

There aren't any wolves in the wild in Britain these days, but in the 9th century they prowled all over the land, ravaging sheep and cattle. To solve the problem, Hywel Dda's successor, Owain, was made to pay the English king a yearly tax of 300 wolves' heads.

After three years, the wolves had been all but wiped out.

This is a 13th-century picture of Hywel Dda from the oldest surviving copy of the Welsh Law Codes.

Royal Dunadd

The royal capital of Dalriada was a hilltop fort at Dunadd.

Near the top of the hill, there's a rock with a footprint carved into it.

Carved footprint

It was used in king-making ceremonies when the new king placed his foot in the footprint as a symbol of his link to the land. Then he was blessed by the Abbot of Iona – the most important religious person in Dalriada.

Dunadd was also home to many highly skilled craftsmen, such as the metalworkers who made this brooch, which may have belonged to a king.

THE BIRTH OF SCOTLAND

The Welsh kingdoms may not always have shared a ruler, but they did have a common culture. The land that would later become Scotland was very different. It was home to four separate groups of people.

The largest group was the Picts, who ruled most of the Highlands. Their main rivals were the Scots in the kingdom of Dalriada. In the Lowlands, the Anglo-Saxon kingdom of Northumbria reached as far as the River Forth, and Strathclyde was occupied by Celtic-speaking Britons. But, there was one thing that would help to bring them all together: the Christian faith.

Monks and monarchs

In 563, an Irish monk named Columba settled in Dalriada and set up a monastery on the Island of Iona. As well as converting many Scots to Christianity, he advised their king, educated his sons and led missions to rival kingdoms – converting them too. Iona became the religious capital of Dalriada, and many early Scottish kings were buried there.

Viking slaughter

By a cruel irony, another thing that thrust the Scottish people together was the force that wreaked destruction on Iona: the Vikings. Between 794 and 805, Viking pirates ransacked Iona several times. The monks fled. The Western Isles, Orkney and the Shetlands were all conquered. On the mainland, the Picts bore the brunt of the Vikings' repeated ferocious attacks. In 839, the entire Pictish royal family was slaughtered.

MacAlpin

A number of local leaders stepped up to claim kingship over the Picts. Among them was Kenneth MacAlpin, who ruled Dalriada from around 839 and was crowned King of the Picts in 843. There were still other claimants who thought they should rule instead. But, by 849, MacAlpin had seen them off and become undisputed King of both the Picts and the Scots.

No one knows exactly how MacAlpin achieved this, but one story tells that he invited his rivals to a great feast. Once they had eaten and drunk their fill, they were tipped from their seats into concealed pits full of spikes, and slain.

A new kingdom

Six kings followed MacAlpin in just four decades. They all died fighting, either among themselves or against the Vikings. Finally, MacAlpin's grandson Constantine II brought some stability to the land. He fought off attacks by the Vikings and the English.

His kingdom came to be known as Alba, but within a century it would be known as Scotland.

KENNETH I
MacAlpin
c.839–858

Ruled both the Picts and the Scots from 843.

CONSTANTINE II
900–943

Spent most of his reign at war with King Athelstan of England, but spent the last ten years of his life as a monk.

Tit for tat

In 934, Athelstan of England invaded Scotland. Constantine held out under siege at Dunnottar Castle (below), but in the end he had to come to terms with the English.

Three years later, they fought again, at the Battle of Brunanburh. Athelstan won, but he didn't try to invade Scotland again.

This is Dunsinane Hill, near Perth,
Shakespeare's setting for MacBeth's defeat by
Malcolm Canmore. At the top, there are the
remains of an ancient hill fort, known locally
as MacBeth's Castle.

The Scottish play

William Shakespeare's
play about MacBeth bears
little resemblance to the
true events. In his version,
MacBeth is cast as a villain
who murders Duncan in
his bed.

The play was written in
1603-6, for James VI of
Scotland and I of England,
who claimed to be descended
from Duncan. Shakespeare
included witches and ghosts
in the play to please James,
who was fascinated by the
supernatural.

TOIL AND TROUBLE

Alba was still a turbulent place, where kings' reigns
were often cut short by violence. To avoid leaving
the kingdom without a ruler, the Scots chose a living
king's heir, or 'tanist', from among all his male relatives.
But Malcolm II wanted only his direct descendants to
succeed him. He named his grandson, Duncan, as his
heir and killed off anyone with a rival claim.

Duncan proved a weak and unpopular monarch.
In 1040, he tried to seize the independent region of
Moray by force. But MacBeth, Earl of Moray,
fought back and won.

The real MacBeth

MacBeth, who had a strong claim to the throne in any
case, made himself King. Far from the villain he has
been made out to be, he brought law and order to the
land, gave generously to the church and even made a
pilgrimage to Rome. But, in August 1057, Duncan's
son, Malcolm Canmore, came for revenge.
MacBeth was killed at the Battle of Lumphanan.

This family tree shows how the Scottish succession often jumped from one branch of the family to another, and that many kings' reigns were very brief.

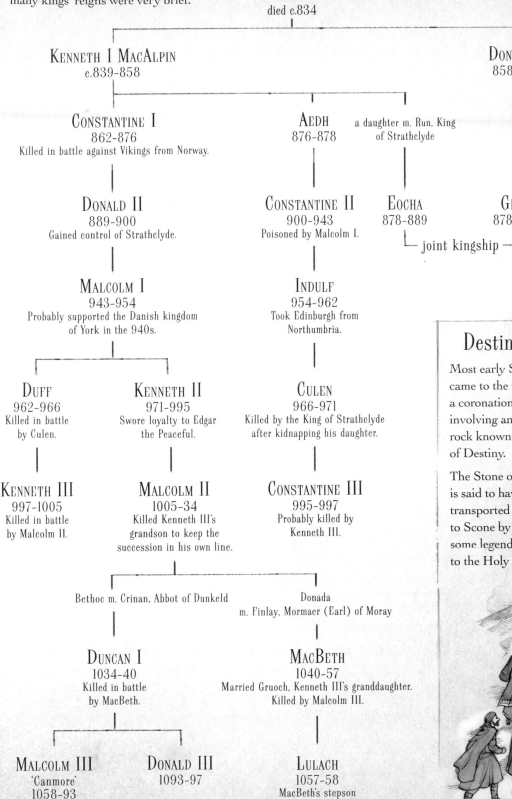

ALPIN
died c.834

KENNETH I MACALPIN
c.839–858

DONALD I
858–862

CONSTANTINE I
862–876
Killed in battle against Vikings from Norway.

AEDH
876–878

a daughter m. Run, King of Strathclyde

DONALD II
889–900
Gained control of Strathclyde.

CONSTANTINE II
900–943
Poisoned by Malcolm I.

EOCHA
878–889

GIRIC
878–889

└─ joint kingship ─┘

MALCOLM I
943–954
Probably supported the Danish kingdom of York in the 940s.

INDULF
954–962
Took Edinburgh from Northumbria.

DUFF
962–966
Killed in battle by Culen.

KENNETH II
971–995
Swore loyalty to Edgar the Peaceful.

CULEN
966–971
Killed by the King of Strathclyde after kidnapping his daughter.

KENNETH III
997–1005
Killed in battle by Malcolm II.

MALCOLM II
1005–34
Killed Kenneth III's grandson to keep the succession in his own line.

CONSTANTINE III
995–997
Probably killed by Kenneth III.

Bethoc m. Crinan, Abbot of Dunkeld

Donada
m. Finlay, Mormaer (Earl) of Moray

DUNCAN I
1034–40
Killed in battle by MacBeth.

MACBETH
1040–57
Married Gruoch, Kenneth III's granddaughter.
Killed by Malcolm III.

MALCOLM III
'Canmore'
1058–93

DONALD III
1093–97

LULACH
1057–58
MacBeth's stepson

Destiny's stone

Most early Scottish kings came to the throne with a coronation ceremony involving an ancient slab of rock known as the Stone of Destiny.

The Stone of Destiny is said to have been transported from Dunadd to Scone by MacAlpin, but some legends trace it back to the Holy Land.

Hill of Tara

In Irish mythology, the Hill of Tara was the place where the first High Kings of Ireland lived and ruled.

At the top of the hill is the Lia Fail, or Stone of Destiny, which was used in the coronation ceremony. Apparently, it would roar three times if the man being crowned was the rightful king.

This aerial photograph shows the remains of the king's fort at the Hill of Tara.

KINGS OF THE HILL

It is difficult to know for certain who the first kings of Ireland really were. The country was populated by Celtic tribes who couldn't read or write. Instead, they passed on stories about their kings, by word of mouth, from generation to generation. These stories weren't written down until centuries later, so facts about the lives of kings have long since become mixed up in myth and legend.

Power levels

It is said that Ireland was ruled by many kings with differing levels of power. At the bottom level, a chief, or 'Ri', oversaw a single tribe. At a higher level, Ireland was split into five territories, known as the Five Fifths, each with its own king.

The most powerful ruler of the five had the title of 'High King', or 'Ard Ri'. He made the other kings swear loyalty to him, and had his base at the Hill of Tara.

Fort of Caelchon – a chief under King Cormac

Banqueting Hall – probably the entrance road to Tara

Fort of the Synods

Mound of the Hostages

Lia Fail (Stone of Destiny)

The Forrad – a public meeting place or court

The House of King Cormac

Legendary kings

According to Irish myths, one of the first high kings was Cormac the Wise. He had a golden cup that broke apart when someone told a lie, and mended itself when it heard the truth.

Another legendary king, Niall of the Nine Hostages, reigned from around the 4th century. He often raided England, and on one trip, brought a Romano-British boy back as a slave. The boy brought Christianity to Ireland, and was later known as St. Patrick.

Battling Fifths

Unlike those in England and Scotland, kings in Ireland didn't follow any line of succession. So, the rulers of the Fifths were frequently fighting each other, trying to seize rival territories. From the late 8th century, they were also fighting the Vikings, who invaded and took over prosperous settlements such as Dublin and Cork.

In the 10th century, Brian Boru became King of Munster, a territory in south west Ireland. A skilled warrior, he quickly gained control of many Irish kingdoms. In just a few years, Brian had overthrown the other rulers in Ireland, including Sitric, the Viking King of Dublin, to claim the title of High King.

Trouble at the top

Although Brian had shot to power, keeping control of the country proved difficult. Soon, rebellions broke out across Ireland, and Brian took his army to fight them, one by one. In 1014, Brian's forces won the Battle of Clontarf, but he was killed there, along with his son.

Hostage taking

A high king ensured loyalty from a rival king by taking one of his close relatives hostage. If the rival remained faithful, the hostage was well looked after. If he didn't, the hostage was killed.

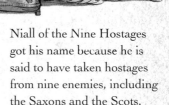

Niall of the Nine Hostages got his name because he is said to have taken hostages from nine enemies, including the Saxons and the Scots.

BRIAN BORU
1002-1014
Born: c.941
Died: April 23, 1014
King of Munster from c.976, Brian skilfully overthrew the other kings of the Five Fifths to become High King of Ireland.

He was killed fighting Viking and Irish rebels at the Battle of Clontarf.

EDWARD II
'the Martyr'
975–978
Murdered while visiting his
half-brother, Ethelred, and
stepmother at Corfe Castle.

ETHELRED
'the Unready'
978–1013 &
1014–1016
Known as 'he Unready'
meaning ill-advised. Spent
most of his reign fighting
Danish Vikings.

EDMUND
'Ironside'
April–November 1016
Ethelred's son, who gained his
nickname because he
was a strong soldier.

KINGS AT WAR

After King Edgar died, in 975, there was much disagreement among the English nobles about who should succeed him. Edgar had been married twice and had a son by each wife. Some nobles wanted the elder son, 12-year-old Edward, to be King. But others backed the younger son, Ethelred, who was nine. Edward was crowned, but the two sides continued to fight, and in 978, he was murdered by his half-brother's supporters. Ethelred became King, but because he didn't take advice from his council, the Witan, he made many mistakes.

A new invasion

To make things worse, Vikings from Denmark began raiding again in the south and east. In 991, they launched a huge invasion, sparking many years of war, as the English and the Danes battled it out for control of England. In the end, the Danish King, Cnut, won, and although he came to the throne by force, he soon gained the respect of the English people.

The Danish fleet that invaded England in 991 was reported to be made up of 93 warships carrying over 2,000 men. This detail from a 10th-century Scandinavian painting shows part of that force.

This timeline describes the main events and characters involved in the long struggle between the English and the Danes at the end of the 10th and the start of the 11th century.

991

Viking forces land in Essex and defeat the English at the Battle of Maldon.

991-1002

Ethelred is forced to pay the Vikings huge sums of money – 'Danegeld' – to stay away.

1002

Ethelred orders the massacre of all Danes living in England, provoking the Danish King, Swein 'Forkbeard', to renew attacks.

SWEIN
'Forkbeard'
1013-1014

The King of Denmark attacked England repeatedly from the 990s and had conquered the land by 1013.

CNUT
1016-1035

Forkbeard's son, who succeeded Edmund Ironside. Cnut was a strong, diplomatic ruler, and his reign was peaceful.

According to a legend, some of Cnut's admirers claimed he had power over the sea. To prove he was only human, the King took his throne to the beach and ordered back the tide. Naturally, the water came in anyway, and Cnut got wet feet.

1013

Swein and his son, Cnut, conquer northern England, and then the rest of the country. Ethelred flees to Normandy.

Spring 1014

Ethelred returns to England and drives Cnut back to Denmark.

February 1014

Swein dies and Cnut is crowned King of England.

Spring 1015

Ethelred's son, Edmund, leads a revolt against his father, making himself ruler in the north of England.

August 1015

Cnut invades northern England again, but Edmund fights him off.

November 1016

Edmund dies and Cnut becomes King of all England.

October 1016

After months of fighting, Cnut defeats Edmund. So many soldiers have been killed on both sides, that they agree to split the kingdom between them.

April 1016

Ethelred dies, and Edmund is crowned King of England.

1017

Cnut marries Ethelred's widow, Emma of Normandy.

1018

England is finally at peace. Cnut dismisses most of his army, keeping only a small force, known as the 'housecarls'.

1035

Cnut dies. He wanted his son, Harthacnut, to succeed him. Unfortunately, things wouldn't go quite as smoothly as he'd hoped...

HAROLD I
'Harefoot'
1037–1040
Born: 1016

Regent from 1035

Cnut's son by his first wife.
Harold seized the throne from
his half-brother, Harthacnut.

HARTHACNUT
1035–1042
Born: 1018

Crowned: 1040

Cnut's son by Emma of
Normandy. His reign was
brief and violent. He died of
convulsions at a wedding.

EDWARD
'the Confessor'
1042–1066
Born: 1004

Crowned: April 3, 1043

Died: January 5, 1066

The last Anglo-Saxon king. After
Edward died, there was a contest
for the throne that ended with
the Norman Conquest.

THE LAST ANGLO-SAXON

When Cnut died in 1035, disputes over who would succeed him brought the peace and security of his reign to an abrupt end. Harthacnut, Cnut's son with his second wife, Ethelred's widow Emma of Normandy, was his chosen heir.

But, while Harthacnut was busy defending his Danish territories, Harold, his half-brother, seized power in England. In 1037, he made himself King.

End of the line

Harthacnut returned to England in 1040, with a fleet of 62 warships, ready to fight his brother. But, Harold had fallen ill and was already dead. So Harthacnut succeeded to the throne, unopposed. As revenge for his brother's treachery, he ordered Harold's body to be dug up and thrown in a bog.

But, Harthacnut's reign didn't last for long. He died suddenly in 1042, unmarried and childless. It was the end of Cnut's dynasty.

Edward returns

Luckily, before he died, Harthacnut had made sure he had named his heir. His elder half-brother, Edward, was the son of Emma of Normandy and Ethelred the Unready. After Cnut defeated Ethelred, Edward had fled to Normandy. He lived there until 1041, when Harthacnut invited him to return to England, and promised him the English throne. As an Anglo-Saxon, Edward had a lot of support among English nobles, and was crowned without opposition.

Earl in control

Edward had never expected to be King, and his passions were hunting and the Church. He gave important jobs to his Norman friends, which didn't go down well with the Anglo-Saxon nobles, especially one named Godwine. By the time Edward was crowned, Godwine was the Earl of Wessex, and had almost as much power as the King. He even persuaded Edward to marry his daughter, Edith.

Westminster

Soon, Edward concentrated less on ruling England, and became involved in a magnificent new building project. He ordered a grand abbey and royal palace to be built to the west of the old Roman city of London.

The abbey was named Westminster Abbey, and the area became a base, or capital, where the King met his advisers, made laws, and dealt with government matters.

The Bayeux Tapestry was made in the 1070s to depict the events around the year 1066. This scene from the tapestry shows Edward issuing orders from his throne.

A saintly king

Edward was regarded as a pious man. A century after his death, he was declared a saint.

It was then that people began to refer to him as 'the Confessor', meaning a person who has led a holy life.

HAROLD II

'Godwinson'

January–October 1066

Born: 1022

Crowned: January 5, 1066

Died: October 14, 1066

Harold seized the English throne after Edward the Confessor died. Just nine months later, he was killed at the Battle of Hastings.

This photograph shows a re-enactment of the Battle of Hastings.

1066 AND ALL THAT

As Edward got older, he gave more and more power to his nobles. When Earl Godwine died, he left control of Wessex to his son, Harold Godwinson, who soon became Edward's closest adviser. The ageing King had no children to succeed him – and Harold most certainly had his eye on the throne.

Succession crisis

Edward died on January 4, 1066, and Harold was crowned the very next day. Popular, charming and a successful army leader, Harold was the obvious choice to become King. His succession was also supported by many English nobles.

Meanwhile, Edward's cousin, William, Duke of Normandy, was mustering his forces. He claimed that Edward had named him as his heir 15 years earlier, and he was determined to seize the crown for himself.

Viking attack

To guard against a Norman attack, Harold posted an army on the south coast. But he was soon facing another threat. The King of Norway, Harald Hardrada, wanted England for himself. In September 1066, he led a fleet of warships up the River Humber, and landed near York, in the north of England.

Harold raced to meet the Vikings, killing Hardrada and defeating his army at Stamford Bridge.

The Battle of Hastings

Three days later, William invaded the south coast with a huge army. Showing amazing stamina, Harold and his exhausted troops marched south. On October 14, they fought the Normans at the Battle of Hastings. Harold was killed, and William became King soon after. The Norman Conquest had begun.

Battling at Stamford Bridge

During the Battle of Stamford Bridge, English and Viking forces were on opposite sides of the river. Any English soldier who tried to cross the bridge was killed by a huge, axe-wielding Viking.

The Viking was only defeated when an English soldier floated under the bridge on a barrel and speared him from below.

A French dynasty

William the Conqueror ruled Normandy, in northern France, before he invaded England and made himself King. So he and his successors are known as the Normans.

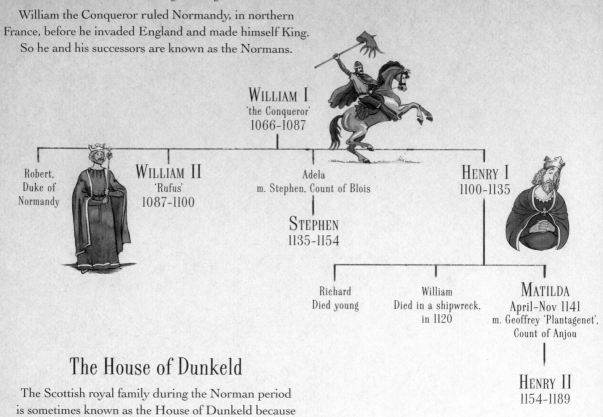

WILLIAM I
'the Conqueror'
1066–1087

Robert,
Duke of
Normandy

WILLIAM II
'Rufus'
1087–1100

Adela
m. Stephen, Count of Blois

STEPHEN
1135–1154

HENRY I
1100–1135

Richard
Died young

William
Died in a shipwreck,
in 1120

MATILDA
April–Nov 1141
m. Geoffrey 'Plantagenet',
Count of Anjou

HENRY II
1154–1189

The House of Dunkeld

The Scottish royal family during the Norman period is sometimes known as the House of Dunkeld because Malcolm Canmore's grandfather was the Abbot of Dunkeld (see page 23).

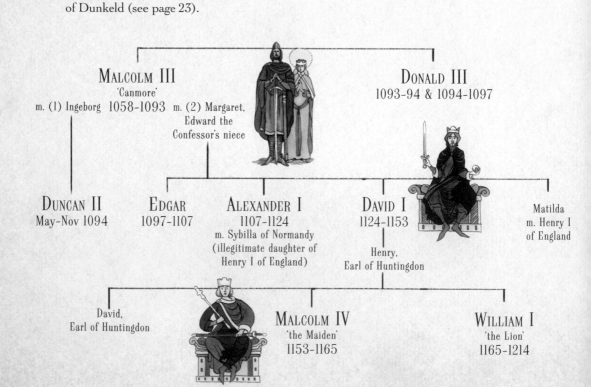

MALCOLM III
'Canmore'
m. (1) Ingeborg 1058–1093 m. (2) Margaret,
Edward the
Confessor's niece

DONALD III
1093–94 & 1094–1097

DUNCAN II
May–Nov 1094

EDGAR
1097–1107

ALEXANDER I
1107–1124
m. Sybilla of Normandy
(illegitimate daughter of
Henry I of England)

DAVID I
1124–1153

Matilda
m. Henry I
of England

Henry,
Earl of Huntingdon

David,
Earl of Huntingdon

MALCOLM IV
'the Maiden'
1153–1165

WILLIAM I
'the Lion'
1165–1214

THE NORMANS

In 1066, William Duke of Normandy invaded
and conquered England. William and his
Norman successors brought French culture
and language to the land, replacing
Anglo-Saxon leaders with a ruling class of
Norman noblemen, and building lots of castles.

The Normans didn't conquer Wales and
Scotland, but they had a strong influence over
them, and often tried to claim overlordship
over the Scots kings.

WILLIAM I

'the Conqueror'
1066-1087

Born: Normandy, 1027

Crowned: Westminster
Abbey, December 25, 1066

Died: September 9, 1087

Duke of Normandy who
conquered England in 1066.
Responsible for compiling the
Domesday Book and building
lots of castles.

This embroidered scene from
the Bayeux Tapestry shows the
moment King Harold was killed
and the Normans won the Battle
of Hastings.

A NORMAN CONQUEROR

William, Duke of Normandy, inherited his title when he was only seven, and was exposed to violent power struggles as people tried to overthrow him. As he grew up, he was keen to assert his own authority. He crushed rebellions, and seized the territories of his rivals.

William was a distant relative of Edward the Confessor. When Edward died, William claimed that Edward had promised him the English throne 15 years earlier. He was determined to fight Harold, who had seized the throne, and was sure he had the skill and might to conquer England.

William's victory

In October 1066, William landed on the south coast of England with 7,000 men and horses, and on October 14, the English and Norman armies clashed near Hastings. Harold's men fought hard, but William's trained archers and knights on horseback quickly overpowered them. Harold was killed, and his frightened soldiers fled the battle scene.

The Normans had won the Battle of Hastings.

Christmas coronation

Marching to London, William and his men brutally slayed anyone who resisted them. Less than three months after invading, on Christmas Day 1066, William was crowned in Westminster Abbey.

Despite his warrior-like personality, William was also a very religious man. He made sure he had the Pope's consent before invading England, and built an abbey at the site of the Battle of Hastings, to commemorate the people who died there.

Fighting back

Even though William had taken the English throne, his conquest of the country was far from over. Anglo-Saxon lords and church leaders were forced to swear allegiance to him, but many tried to rebel. This didn't bother him. Most of the uprisings were small and badly organized, so William simply took his powerful army up and down the country, defeating them one by one.

William's actions earned him the nickname 'William the Conqueror'.

This is a silver penny from the reign of William the Conqueror, showing his portrait.

Portraits from this time aren't very realistic, so we don't know what he really looked like.

This figure below with an arrow in his eye is probably meant to be Harold. But it's unlikely he actually died this way.

Motte and bailey

Many of the first Norman castles were known as *motte and bailey* castles.

A wooden tower, or 'keep', was built on top of a huge, earth mound, known as a 'motte'. The lord and his knights lived in the 'keep'. Servants lived in a fortified area, called a 'bailey', next to it.

Over time, the wooden keeps were replaced by stone ones, some of which are still standing today.

Cardiff Castle was first built in 1091 by the Lord of Gloucester, on the site of an old Roman fort. Positioned on the Welsh border, the lord could easily look out for approaching danger.

WILLIAM'S LEGACY

In the winter of 1069, William faced his most serious challenge yet. The north of England was invaded by a pretender to the throne, Edgar the Aetheling, and many English people soon rose up in support of him. Edgar was an Anglo-Saxon, and a great-nephew of Edward the Confessor.

William hit back ruthlessly, sending troops to destroy everything in their path – houses, crops and livestock – while the terrified locals fled. Thousands of people were killed or died of starvation and cold. It came to be known as the Harrying of the North.

King of the castle

William didn't only use his own army to keep the English people under control. He replaced nearly all English lords with Norman ones, divided up the land between them, and gave them their own set of soldiers.

Each lord also had a castle built. Tall, closely-guarded walls kept the lords inside safe from potential rebellions, and allowed them to keep a look out for approaching enemies.

Norman castles were designed to intimidate – a warning that someone was in charge. William even had his own three-storey castle built as soon as he arrived in London. It was rebuilt in 1077, and is now part of the Tower of London.

Filling two volumes, the Domesday Book is a record of what people owned in William the Conqueror's time. This volume is open at the pages about Norfolk.

Domesday

One of William's main reasons for invading England was to get his hands on the country's wealth. He wanted to find out exactly what people owned and how much money he might be able to get through collecting taxes from them. So, he sent out officials to make a detailed survey of every English county. This information was then written down in a huge book, called the Domesday Book.

Marcher lords

When William conquered England, the Welsh kingdoms were ruled by princes, and Scotland was ruled by King Malcolm III. But, their frontiers weren't fixed. This meant that the bordering areas, or marches, often changed hands. To defend them, William posted his most able lords there, known as marcher lords. In Wales, he encouraged his marcher lords to widen their territories deep into the region.

Counting it up

The Domesday Book gives the details of:

13,418 towns, villages and hamletss

48 castles

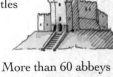

More than 60 abbeys and over 300 local churches

45 vineyards

Hundreds of woodlands, pastures and fisheries

MALCOLM III
'Canmore'
1058-1093
Born: c.1031
Spent much of his reign in conflict with William the Conqueror and his successors.

DONALD III
1093-4 & 1094-7
Born: c.1032
Malcolm's brother.

DUNCAN II
1094
Born: c.1060
Malcolm's son. Released from captivity by William Rufus to overthrow Donald, but died in battle six months later.

EDGAR
1097-1107
Born: c.1073
Malcolm's son. Seized the Scottish throne with the help of the English.

ALEXANDER I
1107-24
Born: c.1079
Malcolm's son. Married to Sybilla, daughter of Henry I of England.

FIGHTING FOR SCOTLAND

William wasn't the only ruler determined to extend his kingdom. While the Norman army was busy dealing with English revolts during the conquest, Malcolm III, King of the Scots, turned this upheaval to his advantage, and invaded England.

Invasions

From 1066 on, Malcolm marched his men into the north of England four times – but was repeatedly driven back by the Normans. In 1072, Malcolm invaded again. This time, William faced him directly, with a large army. Malcolm was forced to swear allegiance to William, and forbidden from attacking again. He also handed over his son Duncan as a hostage. Despite this, Malcolm broke the terms of the treaty and continued to invade England many times.

A lasting legacy

Although previous Scottish kings often had to fight off rivals to the throne, Malcolm's 35-year reign was never challenged. He became known as 'Canmore', meaning 'big head' or 'chief', because his descendants ruled Scotland for the next 250 years.

In 1070, Malcolm married Edward the Confessor's great-niece, Margaret. She gave refuge to many English nobles driven out of England by William, which had a big influence on the Scottish court. For example, to make Margaret and the nobles feel more at home, Malcolm changed the language of the Scots court from Gaelic to English.

Saintly queen

Margaret was a devout Christian. She set up an abbey at Dumfermline and also gave generously to the poor, often feeding orphans from her own plate. She was made a saint after her death in 1250, and a chapel was built in her memory at Edinburgh Castle.

Who will rule next?

In 1093, Malcolm was killed fighting the English at the Battle of Alnwick. Edward, his eldest son and heir, was also killed. Queen Margaret was stricken with grief when she heard the news, and died just a few days later.

Malcolm's younger brother, Donald, was crowned. Around the same time, Malcolm's son Duncan was set free by the English King. With the help of an English army, Duncan seized the Scottish throne from his uncle.

Just a few months later, Donald killed Duncan in battle and became King again. But, another of Malcolm's sons, Edgar, eventually defeated Donald and became King. He was later succeeded by his brother, Alexander.

This is a stained glass window showing Queen Margaret, from the Margaret Chapel in Edinburgh Castle.

Malcolm made Edinburgh his main base and built a stone fort there. The Edinburgh Castle that stands there today was built on top of it.

This early 14th century painting shows William the Conqueror out hunting – *the* pastime for the Normans. They created 22 royal hunting grounds, including the New Forest, where William II was killed in a hunting 'accident'.

WILLIAM II
'Rufus'
1087–1100

Born: c.1060

Crowned: Westminster Abbey, Sept 26, 1087

Died: In a hunting accident, August 2, 1100

William the Conqueror's second son. Known as 'Rufus' (which means 'the red') either because he had red hair or a ruddy complexion.

DEATH AND DISASTER

In 1087, William the Conqueror was badly injured while fighting in Normandy, and died three weeks later. On his death bed, the King set out his final wishes. Robert, his eldest son, would become Duke of Normandy. William, his best-loved and devoted middle son, was to be King of England. Henry, the youngest, got nothing.

Bickering brothers

As soon as he heard the news, William rushed to London to be crowned. But, he and Robert had been rivals since childhood, so the division of power caused problems between them. The two brothers each wanted to control both England and Normandy, and constantly fought over each other's lands.

But, like his father, William was a skilful military leader and tactician. He swiftly put down Robert's supporters in England, then took forces to invade Normandy, forcing his brother to give up some of his territory there.

40

Death in the forest

In August, 1100, William was out hunting with his younger brother, Henry, when he was killed by an arrow. Was it an accident? Henry hadn't been left any land by his father, and he may have planned William's murder so that he could overthrow him. If Henry wasn't responsible for William's death, he quickly turned it to his advantage. Just three days later, he was crowned King.

A cunning king

Henry was clever and ambitious. As soon as he came to power, he abolished some unpopular laws and taxes. This won him the support of the English people. He formed links with Scotland, too, by marrying Malcolm III's daughter, Matilda. Like his brother, Henry waged war on Robert for Normandy, and won. To make sure he was never challenged again, Henry had Robert imprisoned for the rest of his life.

Disaster at sea

In 1120, tragedy struck. Henry's only sons were drowned when their boat, the *White Ship*, sank in the English Channel. Henry was distraught. Who would succeed him now? He wanted it to be his daughter, Matilda, but this was a risky choice. Stephen, Henry's nephew and grandson of William the Conqueror, thought the throne should be his.

King Henry I mourns the death of his two sons in the wreck of the *White Ship*. The tragedy must have had a lasting impact – this painting was made some 200 years after the event.

HENRY I
1100–1135
Born: c.1068

Crowned: Westminster Abbey, August 6, 1100

Died in 1135, of food poisoning, supposedly as a result of eating too many lampreys (water creatures similar to eels).

This portrait of David I of Scotland, on the left, and his grandson and successor, Malcolm IV, is from a manuscript written just after David's death.

DAVID I
1124-1153

Born: c.1084

Died: May 24, 1153

The last, and most successful, of Malcolm Canmore's sons to rule Scotland. Brought up in England, he introduced many Anglo-Norman ways to Scotland.

MALCOLM IV
1153-1165

Born: March 20, 1141

Died: December 9, 1165

David's grandson was only 12 when he became King of Scotland. He later became known as Malcolm 'the Maiden' because he died young and never married.

CHANGE IN SCOTLAND

By the time Alexander I died in 1124, his younger brother David was already a powerful man. Exiled to England by Donald III when he was only nine or ten, David grew up as a noble in the English court. He was a close friend of Henry I, and his marriage to a noblewoman gave him control of important English territories such as Huntingdon and Northampton. Now, David was also going to be King of Scots.

But, David had a rival. Alexander had an illegitimate son, Malcolm, who thought that he should be king. Many people in Scotland resented David's English ways, and rose up in support of Malcolm. However, David had the backing of a trained English army and soon crushed Malcolm and the rebels. He then built castles all over Scotland and appointed lords to keep an eye on his people.

Down to business

Strongly influenced by his time in England, David was keen to introduce Anglo-Norman ways, such as trade and commerce, to Scotland. He encouraged European traders and craftsmen to move to Scotland and form trading settlements, where people gathered to buy and sell their goods. Known as *burghs*, each of these towns was run by a lord who collected a tax on the produce that was sold.

Scottish power

Like his father, Malcolm Canmore, David was determined to extend Scottish rule south. When Henry I died, England was thrown into chaos. David took advantage of the situation and invaded, devastating villages, and killing anyone who resisted him. He only stopped when he had taken important towns, such as Carlisle and Durham.

A young successor

David was in his seventies when Henry, his only son and heir, died. Just a year later, David died, too, and he was succeeded by his 12 year old grandson, Malcolm. Often suffering from ill health, Malcolm died when he was only 24, childless and unmarried.

Scottish coins

The first Scottish coins were pressed or 'minted' during David I's reign. They were made from silver and helped people to put a value on the goods they bought and sold.

David I was a dedicated Christian who set up many monasteries during his reign.

This is Melrose Abbey, which David founded in 1136. Alexander II of Scotland is buried there, as well as the embalmed heart of Robert the Bruce.

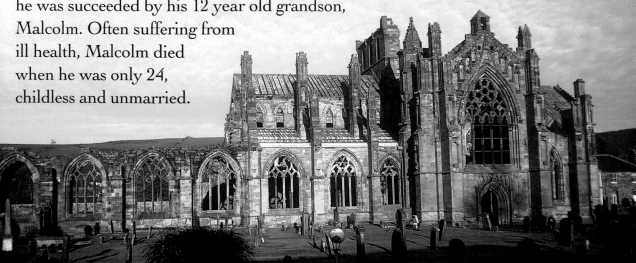

STEPHEN
1135–1154

Born: c.1097

Seized the throne:
December 22, 1135

Deposed: April 7, 1141

Restored to the throne:
November 1, 1141

Died: October 25, 1154

William the Conqueror's
grandson. Civil war raged
between Stephen and his cousin,
Matilda, for most of his reign.

"By his good nature
and the way he jested
and enjoyed himself
... Stephen earned
an affection that can
hardly be imagined."

William of Malmesbury,
a writer from the time,
describes Stephen's style
of kingship.

THE ANARCHY

After the death of his only sons in the *White Ship* disaster, Henry I desperately tried to ensure that his daughter, Matilda, would succeed him, even making his lords swear that they would be loyal to her. But, as soon as Henry died, his nephew, Stephen, rushed to London to seize power, while Matilda was still in France. He was crowned King of England on 22 December, just three weeks after Henry's death.

Stephen as king

Many Norman lords were actually pleased that Stephen was King. They were uneasy about being ruled by a woman, as it was unusual for women to hold postitions of authority. What's more, Matilda was married to a French lord, Geoffrey of Anjou. The Normans were long-standing enemies of the people of Anjou, known as Angevins, and they didn't like the idea of Geoffrey having influence over them. Despite this, Stephen's hold on power was far from secure. In 1138, Matilda landed in England, determined to fight for the throne.

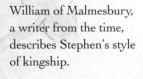

This is Stephen. It is said
that he remained kind,
good-natured and cheerful
throughout the civil war.

Civil war

Soon, rebellions broke out in support of Matilda, forcing Stephen into battle on several fronts at once. Matilda's husband, Geoffrey, attacked Normandy, David I of Scotland marched into northern England, and the Welsh rose up against their Norman rulers. The Norman territories were plunged into a civil war, known as the Anarchy.

No winners

Stephen had the upper hand many times during the war, but he didn't always get things right. At the beginning of the war, he captured Matilda, but she was able to persuade him to let her go. To try to stop the fighting, he also rashly agreed to give Normandy to Geoffrey of Anjou.

Matilda made mistakes, too. In April 1141, she defeated Stephen in battle and marched into London. But, she argued with officials and church leaders, and was driven out of the city, without being crowned.

A new dynasty

Finally, in 1148, Matilda returned to France. But she wasn't entirely defeated. In 1153, Stephen's son, Eustace, died. Stephen was forced to accept Matilda's son, Henry, as his heir.

A new dynasty was set to inherit the English throne.

MATILDA
'The Empress'
April–November 1141

Born: London,
February, 1102

Ascended to the throne:
December 22, 1135

Crowned: never

Seized the throne:
April–November, 1141

Died: Normandy, 1167

Daughter of Henry I
of England and Matilda
of Scotland she and Stephen
fought for the throne in
an 18-year civil war .

This portrait of Matilda is from a 15th century manuscript.

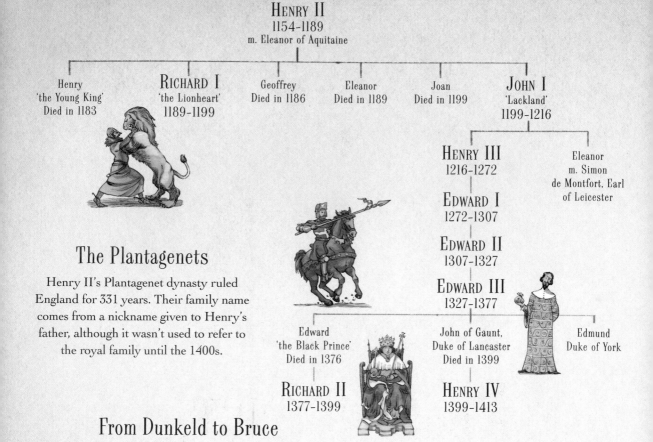

HENRY II
1154-1189
m. Eleanor of Aquitaine

Henry 'the Young King' Died in 1183	RICHARD I 'the Lionheart' 1189-1199	Geoffrey Died in 1186	Eleanor Died in 1189	Joan Died in 1199	JOHN I 'Lackland' 1199-1216

HENRY III
1216-1272

Eleanor
m. Simon
de Montfort, Earl
of Leicester

EDWARD I
1272-1307

EDWARD II
1307-1327

EDWARD III
1327-1377

The Plantagenets

Henry II's Plantagenet dynasty ruled England for 331 years. Their family name comes from a nickname given to Henry's father, although it wasn't used to refer to the royal family until the 1400s.

Edward
'the Black Prince'
Died in 1376

John of Gaunt,
Duke of Lancaster
Died in 1399

Edmund
Duke of York

RICHARD II
1377-1399

HENRY IV
1399-1413

From Dunkeld to Bruce

In 1290, the Dunkeld dynasty came to an end, leaving the Scots with no obvious heir to the throne. Years of warfare and instability followed, but eventually Robert the Bruce's line restored a lasting monarchy to Scotland.

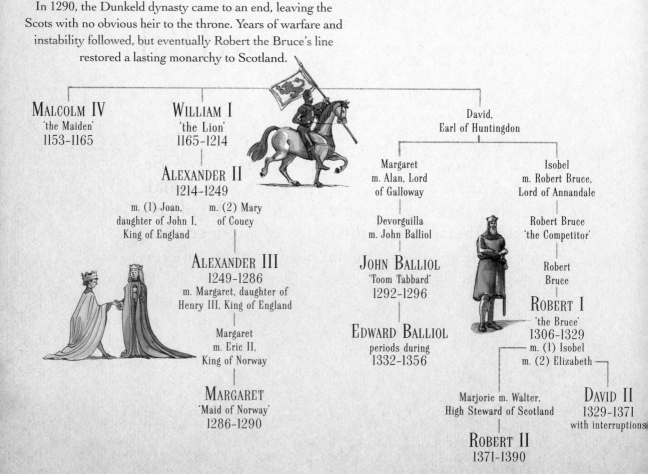

MALCOLM IV
'the Maiden'
1153-1165

WILLIAM I
'the Lion'
1165-1214

David,
Earl of Huntingdon

ALEXANDER II
1214-1249

Margaret
m. Alan, Lord
of Galloway

Isobel
m. Robert Bruce,
Lord of Annandale

m. (1) Joan,
daughter of John I,
King of England

m. (2) Mary
of Coucy

Devorguilla
m. John Balliol

Robert Bruce
'the Competitor'

ALEXANDER III
1249-1286
m. Margaret, daughter of
Henry III, King of England

JOHN BALLIOL
'Toom Tabbard'
1292-1296

Robert
Bruce

Margaret
m. Eric II,
King of Norway

EDWARD BALLIOL
periods during
1332-1356

ROBERT I
'the Bruce'
1306-1329
m. (1) Isobel
m. (2) Elizabeth

MARGARET
'Maid of Norway'
1286-1290

Marjorie m. Walter,
High Steward of Scotland

DAVID II
1329-1371
with interruptions

ROBERT II
1371-1390

PLANTAGENET, BALLIOL & BRUCE

Kingship in the Middle Ages was very
precarious. This was an era when strong kings
could be all-powerful, conquering new territories
and amassing great fortunes. But all this could
easily be lost by weaker monarchs who often
found themselves at the mercy of stronger ones,
or facing rebellions by ambitious nobles or even
by disgruntled peasants.

THE FIRST PLANTAGENET

By the time Henry II became King of England, he had already inherited vast swathes of French land from his father and wife. Before long, he would claim overlordship of Wales and Scotland, later invading Ireland and claiming that as part of his domain too.

Intelligent, passionate and energetic, with a fearsome temper, Henry was arguably the most powerful ruler in Europe at the time, and the first in a line of Kings that would rule in England until 1485.

Castle breaker

Henry's first task was to restore royal authority after the years of civil war that had gone before. He tore down castles built by rebel nobles, earning himself the nickname 'Castle breaker'. He hired extra troops with money he raised through 'scutage', a tax nobles had to pay instead of providing military service.

HENRY II
1154–1189

Born: Anjou, France, 1133

Crowned: Westminster Abbey, December 19, 1154

Died: Chinon Castle, France, July 6, 1189

The first Plantagenet King of England, Henry ruled more French lands than the King of France. He's best known for arguing with Thomas Becket, which resulted in Becket being murdered.

The name Plantagenet comes from 'planta genista' — a yellow broom flower that Henry's father often wore in his hat.

Henry rides out in front of his daughter and his wife, Eleanor of Aquitaine, followed by his sons. This is part of a wall painting from a chapel in Chinon, in central France.

Henry built a splendid castle at Chinon. It became one of his main residences, and was where he died.

Law maker

One of the main ways Henry enforced his rule was by reorganizing the legal system in England. He produced a new set of laws that many lawyers now see as the basis of today's English Common Law. He also set up new law courts, and introduced trials by jury.

Defender of the realm

Henry worked hard to control and defend his empire, spending much of his time on the move. During his 35-year reign, he crossed the English Channel as many as 28 times, and preferred wearing practical riding gear to ceremonial robes.

The later years of his reign were marred by conflict within his own family. His sons rose against him, angry about the way he planned to split his territories between them in his will. They were encouraged by their fiery mother, Henry's estranged wife, Eleanor of Aquitaine, along with Philip II of France.

Henry's no-nonsense approach to kingship paid off in the end. Despite threats from all sides, by the time he died, his kingdom was still intact.

Murder in the Cathedral

Henry appointed his friend, Thomas Becket, as Archbishop of Canterbury. But they fell out over how much power the King should have over the Church.

After one argument, Henry yelled, "Will no one rid me of this troublesome priest?"

Four knights overheard him, rode to Canterbury and murdered Becket in the Cathedral.

Henry claimed his knights had misunderstood him. He even walked barefoot to Canterbury as penance.

THE CRUSADER KING

A skilled warrior knight, Henry II's son, Richard I, was handsome and athletic, with all the makings of a legendary hero. Even before he became King, he was nicknamed 'the Lionheart' because of his reputation as a brave fighter.

Off to war

In 1187, the Pope announced a religious war, or Crusade, to capture Jerusalem from the Muslim leader, Salah al-Din, or Saladin. Henry II and Richard both signed up, but Henry died in 1189 before he could go.

Richard was crowned, then headed for Jerusalem. He won several battles, although he failed to take Jerusalem. But, in 1192, news arrived that Richard's brother John had started a rebellion back in England.

A royal ransom

Richard set sail for England, but the journey was a disaster. He was captured in Austria, and held prisoner for two years by Emperor Henry VI. The English had to pay a crippling ransom for his release.

Meanwhile, Philip II of France had seized some of Richard's French territory. As soon as he was freed, Richard went to France. He won back his lands, but was wounded in the fighting. On April 6, 1199, Richard died of his injury, and was succeeded by his younger brother, John.

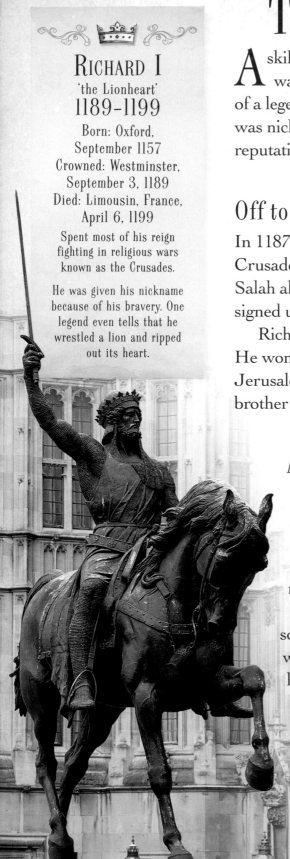

This statue of Richard the Lionheart stands outside the Palace of Westminster in London.

RICHARD I

'the Lionheart'

1189–1199

Born: Oxford,
September 1157
Crowned: Westminster,
September 3, 1189
Died: Limousin, France,
April 6, 1199

Spent most of his reign fighting in religious wars known as the Crusades.

He was given his nickname because of his bravery. One legend even tells that he wrestled a lion and ripped out its heart.

King John hunting a stag

JOHN
1199–1216
'Lackland'

Born: Oxford, 1166

Crowned: Westminster Abbey, May 1199

Died: October 18, 1216

Richard the Lionheart's younger brother. Signed a document known as *Magna Carter* in order to end a revolt among his nobles.

King John apparently lost his crown jewels in the Wash, between Norfolk and Lincolnshire, when he was caught out by the tide.

BAD KING JOHN

John's reign started badly and went downhill from there. He lost his northern French lands to Philip II of France, and angered English nobles by imposing heavy scutage and other taxes on them. John also argued with the Pope, who cast him out of the Church and suspended all church services in England.

By May 1215, the English nobles had lost patience. They raised an army against the King and forced him to sign *Magna Carta*, an agreement protecting people's lives, property and their rights to justice, and promising no illegal taxes. When John tried to back out of it, the nobles invited Louis, Philip II's heir, to London to take over. Louis landed in May 1216, and John fled. He died, on the run, on October 19.

Robin Hood

Tales of Robin Hood refer to Richard the Lionheart and King John, who appears as a villain.

According to legends, Robin Hood was an outlaw who lived with a band of thieves in Sherwood Forest, Nottingham. They stole from the rich to give to the poor.

The stories are probably based on the lives of several real outlaws, over many years, including one named Robert Hood.

WILLIAM I
'the Lion'
1165-1214

Born: 1143

Crowned: Scone, December 24, 1165

Died: Stirling Castle, December 4, 1214

The first Scots King to use the Lion Rampant as his coat of arms. This symbol is still part of the British monarch's coat of arms today.

ALEXANDER II
1214-1249

Born: August 24, 1198

Crowned: Scone, December 6, 1214

Died: Island of Kerrera, July 6, 1249

Alexander backed the English nobles who rebelled against King John, but later made peace with the English, marrying John's daughter, Joan.

ALEXANDER III
1249-1286

Born: September 4, 1241

Crowned: Scone, July 13, 1249

Died: Killed in a riding accident, March 19, 1228

An energetic ruler who took control of the Western Isles and the Isle of Man from the King of Norway.

THE LAST DUNKELDS

Red-headed and powerfully built, David I's grandson, William the Lion, was a born fighter. He began his reign on good terms with Henry II of England, but this changed in 1174. While Henry was busy fighting off his sons' attempts to overthrow him, William invaded Northumberland.

It was a humiliating failure. William was thrown from his horse and captured. According to one report, he was then taken to Henry II, "with his feet shackled beneath the belly of a horse". The Scottish King was forced to accept Henry as his overlord, and English troops were sent to occupy Scotland.

Later, William bought back his independence from Henry's successor, Richard the Lionheart, who needed money for his Crusades.

Long-lived King William

During his reign of nearly 50 years, William proved to be more than just a fighter. He founded Arbroath Abbey, and fostered good relations with Church leaders. As a result, the Pope granted the Scottish Church independence from the Church in England. William died naturally, aged 71 – a rare achievement for a medieval Scottish king.

Teen rebel

William's son, Alexander II, had been knighted by King John when he was 13, but when he became King two years later, in 1214, he sided with the English nobles who were rebelling against John.

Settling differences

Alexander was much more co-operative with King John's successor, Henry III, and even married his sister, Joan, in 1221. Later, Alexander agreed to drop Scottish claims to Northumberland and other parts of northern England, in return for peace.

Highlands and islands

Next, Alexander set out to conquer the Western Isles, where local chiefs looked to the King of Norway as their overlord. But, he fell ill and died on the way.

Alexander II's son was only seven when he became Alexander III. But as soon as he was old enough, he took up his father's campaign. In 1263, he defeated King Haakon of Norway, and by 1266, the Western Isles and the Isle of Man were in Scottish hands.

Alexander III's reign brought prosperity and peace to Scotland. But that was shattered one stormy night, when the King fell from his horse and died, plunging Scotland into chaos.

In this illustration of Alexander III's coronation, the royal poet proclaims, *benach de re albane alex mac alex* – Gaelic for 'God bless the King of Scotland Alex son of Alex'.

Lords of the Isles

The people of the Western Isles of Scotland remained semi-independent from the kings of Scotland even after Alexander III.

The islanders, many of whom were descended from Vikings, were powerful, seafaring people who used 'birlins', boats based on Viking longships, for war and trading.

HENRY III
1216–1272

Born: Winchester,
October 1, 1207

Crowned: Gloucester
Cathedral, October 28,
1216

Died: Westminster,
November 16, 1272

Like his father, King John,
Henry III faced a rebellion from
his nobles. It was during his reign
that England's first Parliament
was called.

Henry's zoo

Henry transformed the
Tower of London, which
was first built for William
the Conqueror. He had new
defensive stone walls added
and extended the royal
quarters there.

During his reign, the Tower
also became home to lions, a
polar bear and an elephant
– exotic gifts to Henry from
foreign rulers.

The polar bear was kept on
a long chain so it could swim
and catch fish in the River
Thames without escaping.

HENRY OF WINCHESTER

England was in the grip of a civil war when Henry
became King in October 1216. In May of that
year, rebels fighting King John, had invited Prince
Louis of France to take control. Since then, French and
rebel forces had gained control of a third of the country.

If John hadn't died, Louis might have been crowned
King of England. But the nobles had nothing against
John's nine-year-old heir, Henry III. They rallied
behind the young King and his regent, William Marshal,
and drove Louis and the French forces back to France.

Tensions mount

The early years of Henry III's reign were relatively
peaceful. But, in 1227, he took over for himself. Many
nobles became resentful when Henry ignored their
advice and gave government jobs to his friends,
and to relatives of his French wife and mother.

From bad to wars

To make things worse, Henry imposed heavy taxes to pay for costly, and unsuccessful, campaigns in Wales and France. When he announced a plan to make his son King of Sicily, the nobles decided they'd had enough.

In 1258, they forced him to sign the Provisions of Oxford, an agreement that the King would call a Great Council of nobles to help him decide all government matters, and he would call Parliament every three years.

Henry soon went back on his word, and civil war broke out again. Led by Simon de Montfort, Earl of Leicester, the nobles defeated royal troops in 1264 at the Battle of Lewes. Henry III and his son Edward were thrown in prison, and de Montfort ruled instead.

Henry's legacy

But Prince Edward escaped and raised an army. In 1265, he defeated the nobles at the Battle of Evesham. De Montfort was killed and Henry returned to power.

Henry was King for 56 years. He was fascinated by Edward the Confessor, and devoted many years to rebuilding Westminster Abbey in the spectacular gothic style tat still stands today, and erecting a shrine to the Confessor there. He died in November 1272, and was buried in the Abbey.

Rebel Earl

Simon de Montfort seems an unlikely English rebel. He was born in France, where he spent much of his time. In 1238, he married Henry's sister, Eleanor.

In 1261, he fell out with Henry, and went to France, returning two years later to lead the nobles in a revolt.

In 1264, he defeated the King and called his own Parliament. For the first time, 'commoners' (knights and important townsmen) were invited as well as nobles. This marked the origins of the House of Commons.

De Montfort's rule didn't last long. In 1265, he was defeated and killed by royal forces at the Battle of Evesham.

This illustration shows how his body was chopped up on the battlefield at Evesham.

EDWARD I
1272-1307
'Longshanks'

Born: June 17, 1239

Crowned: Westminster,
August 19, 1274

Died: July 7, 1307

Edward was nicknamed
'Longshanks' because he
was over 6ft (2m) tall. He
conquered the Welsh, and spent
most of his reign trying to
conquer the Scots — earning
him another nickname,
'Hammer of the Scots'.

HAMMER OF THE SCOTS

E dward I was a determined fighter and a clever
politician. In his youth, he went on a Crusade to
the Holy Land, and as King, his warrior spirit inspired
awe and respect among his subjects — and his enemies.

Profit and persecution

Edward took steps to strengthen royal power and to
increase his income. Overseas, he fought to secure his
lands in France, particularly Gascony. At home, he
reformed many laws to make them less complicated, he
replaced corrupt officials, and he reclaimed lands that
had been taken from his father by rebellious nobles.

In 1275, Edward forbade all Jews in England from
making a profit by money-lending, and in 1290 he
expelled them from the country, seizing their property.

Power through Parliament

Edward always consulted Parliament when he
wanted to raise taxes, but he made it
clear that he was in charge. In 1275,
and from 1295, his Parliament
included two representatives from
every town and two knights from
every county (commoners) as
well as nobles and churchmen
(lords). Almost all future
Parliaments were based on this
so-called 'Model Parliament'.

Edward I crowns his son
Prince of Wales in 1301.

Llywelyn of Wales

At this time, Wales consisted of several small territories, each ruled by a prince. The most powerful of them was Llywelyn ap Gruffydd (pronounced Griffith) who had taken the title Prince of Wales. After Llywelyn repeatedly refused to recognize him as his overlord, Edward invaded in 1277. Llywelyn was forced to sign a peace treaty and stripped of many of his lands.

But in 1282 an uprising in Wales led Edward to invade again, this time to conquer. Llywelyn was killed in battle and the Welsh surrendered.

Taking Wales

In 1284, Wales officially became part of England. To defend his newly-won territory, Edward had a series of stone castles built. Thanks to these, ten years later, a further uprising was swiftly defeated.

In 1301, Edward made his son Prince of Wales. Since then this title has been given to all male heirs to the English (or British) throne.

Fighting Scotland

He may have taken Wales, but the Scots refused to accept Edward as their overlord. In 1296, he led a force of 25,000 men into Scotland. He won a crushing victory, but the Scots refused to surrender completely.

Edward never achieved his goal. In 1307, he died on his way to fight the Scots again. At his request, the Latin inscription on his tombstone reads, *Hic est Edwardus Primus Scottorum Malleus* – "Here lies Edward I the Hammer of the Scots".

A medieval romance

Edward may have been a tough ruler, but he had a tender side too. In 1290, his wife, Eleanor of Castile, died near Lincoln.

He said, "In life I loved her dearly, nor can I cease to love her in death."

Her body was carried to Westminster to be buried and Edward had a series of 12 ornate crosses built at every stop on the way.

Three original 'Eleanor Crosses' are still standing today, at Northampton, Geddington and Waltham Cross, and a replica stands at Charing Cross, London.

These statues of Edward and Eleanor are from Lincoln Cathedral.

MARGARET

'the Maid of Norway'

1286-1290

Born: 1283

Crowned: Never

Died: Orkney, 1290

Margaret's parents were King Erik II of Norway and Margaret, daughter of Alexander III. She succeeded her grandfather, but died before she ever reached Scotland.

JOHN BALLIOL

'Toom Tabbard'

1292-1296

Born: c.1249

Crowned: Scone, November 30, 1292

Died: Normandy, 1313

Great-great-great-grandson of David I, John Balliol was chosen by Edward I of England to be King of Scotland. He was nicknamed 'Toom Tabbard' — meaning empty coat — because he lacked real authority.

John Balliol swears his loyalty to Edward I of England after he is chosen as the new King of Scotland.

THE GREAT CAUSE

After the tragic, accidental death of Alexander III in 1286, Scotland was governed by a group of leading nobles and bishops known as the Guardians of Scotland. The King's only heir was his four-year-old granddaughter, Margaret. In 1290, she set sail from her home in Norway to be crowned Queen in Scotland. But, sadly, Margaret died on the way.

The competitors

More than a dozen competitors stepped forward to claim the throne in what became known as the 'Great Cause'. Two leading candidates emerged: Robert Bruce and John Balliol. Both were descended from daughters of David, the younger brother of William the Lion.

Edward steps in

Fearing the country was on the brink of civil war, the Guardians asked King Edward I of England to adjudicate. Edward chose Balliol.

But it soon became clear that Balliol, who had accepted the English King as his overlord, had very little authority of his own. Edward began interfering with Scottish legal cases, and demanding money and soldiers to fight for him in France.

Friends and enemies

In 1295, the Guardians of Scotland made a treaty with the King of France to help them throw Edward off. This was the start of the Auld Alliance – a long-standing friendship between Scotland and France. It was also a declaration of war against England, and the start of the Scottish Wars of Independence.

Fighting for Scotland

Edward's response was a swift and brutal invasion. In 1296, his troops ravaged southern Scotland. Forced to surrender, Balliol was taken prisoner and later exiled to France for the rest of his life.

Balliol's crown and the Stone of Destiny, on which Scottish kings had been crowned since the 9th century, were seized and taken to London. Edward's message was clear: he was in charge.

But the Scots battled on without a monarch. Edward mounted attacks every summer, and the Scots fought back, each side trying to wear down the other. In 1304, the Scottish nobles finally accepted defeat.

William Wallace

The towering Wallace Monument (above) outside Stirling celebrates William Wallace as a national hero.

Wallace was a nobleman, and one of the Guardians of Scotland. In 1297, he led the Scots to victory against the English at the Battle of Stirling Bridge.

A year later, the English defeated them at the Battle of Falkirk but Wallace refused to surrender.

He continued to fight until 1305 when he was captured, taken to London, and hanged, drawn and quartered.

BRUCE AND FREEDOM

Robert the Bruce inherited his claim to the Scottish throne from his grandfather, and namesake, who had competed with John Balliol for the throne in 1290.

At the start of the Wars of Independence, Bruce fought for Edward I. But he soon switched sides and joined forces with William Wallace.

In 1306, he had himself crowned at Scone, having first murdered his main rival to the throne, Balliol's nephew, John Comyn. But, just three months later, he was defeated by English forces and went into hiding.

This modern statue of Robert the Bruce looks over the site of the Battle of Bannockburn, near Stirling.

Fought in July, 1314, it was a great victory for the Scots against the English.

Fighting back

The following spring, Edward I died, and Bruce immediately launched attacks on English forces in Scotland, often using guerrilla tactics. Meanwhile, he also disposed of his Scottish rivals. By 1314, he had control of all but southeast Scotland. But Stirling Castle was still under English occupation, and Bruce wanted it back.

"Get all ready for battle
For fear of death we shall not fail,
Nor shall any effort be refused
Till we have made our country free!"

Robert the Bruce addresses his troops the night before the Battle of Bannockburn in a poem written around 1380 by the royal poet, John Barbour.

Bannockburn

Edward II of England led a huge army to Scotland to confront Bruce. On June 23, 1314, the two forces met, outside Stirling, at the Battle of Bannockburn. Despite being outnumbered three to one, the battle was a major victory for the Scots. Stirling Castle was back in Scottish hands, and Bruce went on to take Berwick, in 1318. But Edward II still refused to give up his claim to overlordship of Scotland.

Declaration of independence

On April 6, 1320, the Abbot of Arbroath wrote a letter to the Pope on behalf of the Scottish nobles. Probably the most important document in Scotland's history, the letter declared the nation's independence.

The Declaration of Arbroath, as it is now known, also contained a stern warning for Robert the Bruce. If he failed to defend his people's independence, they would, "make someone else our king".

Peace at last

The Pope responded in 1324, recognizing Robert the Bruce as King of an independent Scotland, but it wasn't until 1328, that the English finally followed suit.

Robert the Bruce had achieved his goal, but by this time his health was failing. He died on June 7, 1329, aged 54. His body was buried at Dunfermline Abbey. Following the King's dying wish, one of his knights set off for the Holy Land to bury his heart there. The knight was killed in fighting on the way, but the heart was returned to Scotland and buried at Melrose Abbey.

ROBERT I
'the Bruce'
1306-1329

Born: July 11, 1274

Crowned: March 27, 1306

Died: Possibly of leprosy, June 7, 1329

Buried: Dunfermline Abbey (but his heart is buried at Melrose Abbey)

A great military leader, Robert the Bruce eventually forced the English kings to recognize Scottish independence.

According to a legend, after one defeat, Robert went on the run. He hid in a cave, where he watched a spider try again and again to spin a web until it finally succeeded. This inspired him to keep fighting.

"...never will we on any conditions be brought under English rule. It is in truth not for glory, nor riches, nor honours that we are fighting, but for freedom."

The Declaration of Arbroath, 1320.

EDWARD THE FOP

Edward II was tall, fair and good-looking, just like his father, Edward I. But that's where the similarities ended. He inherited a war with Scotland, which he lost, and a stable, prosperous kingdom, which he left in disarray.

This marble sculpture of Edward II, flanked by two angels, is from his tomb in Gloucester Cathedral.

EDWARD II
1307–1327

Born: Caernarfon, April 25, 1284

Crowned: Westminster, February 25, 1308

Married: Isabella, 'the She-Wolf' of France

Died: Berkley Castle, September 21, 1327

Buried: Gloucester Cathedral

Forced from the throne and imprisoned by his wife, Isabella of France, who was also most likely responsible for his gruesome murder with a hot poker.

The King's cronies

Foppish, feckless and pleasure-seeking, Edward had little interest in the business of government or in achieving military glory. He infuriated his leading nobles by ignoring their advice and filling the court with his friends.

One friendship in particular, with a knight named Piers Gaveston, caused friction from the start. Less than a month after he came to the throne, Edward made Gaveston Duke of Cornwall, a title previously reserved for the eldest son of a king.

Trouble and strife

In 1308, Edward further insulted his nobles by leaving Gaveston in charge of the country while he went to France to be married. His wife was Isabella, daughter of the King of France. She was widely-admired for her intelligence and beauty, but was often neglected by her husband.

Edward's friendship with Gaveston was causing trouble at court. The King's cousin Thomas Lancaster stepped in. In 1310, he formed a council of nobles, the Lords Ordainers. They effectively took over the government and eventually executed Gaveston.

Civil war

But Edward was soon showering gifts of land and titles on another friend, Hugh Despenser. The next decade was dominated by a fierce power struggle between Lancaster and Despenser, which led to a civil war.

In 1321, Lancaster joined forces with another powerful noble named Roger Mortimer. Together, they forced Edward to banish Despenser. But Edward fought back the following year. He executed Lancaster, imprisoned Mortimer and brought back Despenser.

A grisly end

Queen Isabella finally lost patience with Edward. He, in turn, began calling her 'the She-Wolf' of France. She left for France and was joined by Mortimer, who had escaped from prison. They built up an army and invaded England in September 1326.

Edward was imprisoned and his son declared King. The following September, Mortimer had Edward gruesomely murdered with a hot poker.

A woman scorned

When she seized power, Queen Isabella took revenge on her enemies, including her husband's friend, Hugh Despenser, who was horribly put to death.

In this 15th-century painting, clerics welcome Queen Isabella and her son, the future Edward III, to Oxford in 1327.

EDWARD III
1327-1377

Born: Windsor Castle,
November 13, 1312

Crowned: Westminster,
January 29, 1327

Married: Philippa
of Hainault

Died: Sheen Palace,
Surrey, June 21, 1377
from a stroke

A warrior king who believed
he was the rightful King
of France, and started the
Hundred Years' War over
his claim.

Edward changed his coat of
arms to include the fleur de
lys (lillies) of
France alongside
the three lions
of England.

The Black Prince kneels
before his father,
Edward III.

FIGHTING FOR FRANCE

After deposing her husband, and having him murdered, Queen Isabella installed herself as regent for her 14-year-old son, Edward III.

But Edward was strong-willed, confident and determined. At the age of 17, he banished Isabella, had her friend, Roger Mortimer, executed for treason and began to rule for himself. He restored order to the country, dignity to the royal court, and repaired relations with his nobles.

Conquest in mind

Edward was determined to regain the kind of power held by his predecessors, Henry II and Edward I. In 1333, he invaded Scotland, and soon defeated Robert the Bruce's son, David II.

Next, Edward set his sights on France. His mother was the sister of Charles IV of France. In 1328, Charles died and was succeeded by his cousin, Philip. But Edward believed the French throne was rightfully his.

A century of conflict

In 1337, Edward announced his claim to the French throne, and declared war. The fighting would continue, on and off, until 1453 and so it is now known as the Hundred Years' War.

Edward was a formidable general. He won a string of victories, at Sluys in 1340, Crécy in 1346, Calais in 1347 and Poitiers in 1356. During the war, his son, known as the Black Prince, also proved to be a fearsome warrior.

Crécy

The Battle of Crécy was a massive victory for the English because they had the upper hand when it came to tactics and equipment.

The English used longbows, which were lighter and shot arrows faster than the crossbows used by the French. This stopped the French cavalry charge in its tracks.

This 15th-century illustration of the battle shows English longbowmen on the right and French crossbowmen on the left.

The Black Death

In the midst of the wars, a temporary truce was called, as a deadly plague devastated Britain and Europe. Known as the Black Death, the plague wiped out more than a third of the population by 1349. This, and smaller outbreaks in 1361 and 1375, led to a shortage of workers, causing enormous social upheaval.

A reversal of fortunes

By the time Edward III died in 1377, the French had taken back a lot of their lands, and the high cost of the fighting had made him unpopular with his nobles and with Parliament. On top of that, the King had tried to fix wages and prices to pre-plague levels. This contributed to growing discontent among workers and peasants, and would soon lead to unrest.

Order of the Garter

In 1348, Edward III founded the Order of the Garter, a society of the monarch's most important knights.

Members of the Order wear a garter and a badge that shows St. George and the dragon surrounded by the motto, 'HONI SOIT QUI MAL Y PENSE' – which means 'shame on him that thinks evil of it'.

David II of Scotland, in red, shakes hands to make peace with Edward III of England in this illustration from a 14th century manuscript.

The shields above the kings show their coats of arms.

Potty trouble

Royal weddings were nearly always arranged for political reasons, often regardless of the ages of the bride and groom.

Even so, there were raised eyebrows when David, aged four, soiled himself during his wedding to Edward II's daughter, Joanna, aged seven.

BRUCE VS. BALLIOL

Poor David II was only three when his mother died, four when he was married to Edward II's seven-year-old daughter, and five when he succeeded his father, Robert the Bruce, as King of Scotland. He even had a small sceptre made specially for his coronation.

The Balliols, with the backing of Edward III of England, lost no time in claiming the throne for themselves. When David II was ten, he was forced into exile, leaving his 17-year-old nephew Robert Stewart to fight for his cause.

Decades of fighting followed, but eventually it would be the Stewarts who inherited the throne.

This timeline shows some of the main events in the dynastic struggles in Scotland between the Bruces and the Balliols.

NOVEMBER 1331
David II and Queen Joanna are crowned at Scone.

AUGUST 1332
With English support, Edward Balliol invades Scotland and defeats royal troops at the Battle of Dupplin Moor.

SEPTEMBER 1332
Edward Balliol is crowned King of Scots, but driven out of Scotland by David's supporters three months later.

1335
Balliol returns to Scotland. He calls a parliament in Edinburgh but he fails to gain control of the whole country.

JULY 1333
Edward III of England defeats the Scots at the Battle of Halidon Hill. David and Joanna flee to France, and stay there until 1341.

OCTOBER 1346
David invades England but is defeated at the Battle of Neville's Cross, near Durham.

DAVID II
1329-1371
with interruptions
Born: March 5, 1324
Crowned: Scone, November 24, 1331
Died: Edinburgh Castle, February 22, 1371

The son of Robert the Bruce, he became King when he was five. His reign was dominated by civil war.

EDWARD BALLIOL
periods during
1332-56
Born: July 11, 1274
Crowned: Scone, September 24, 1332
Died: 1364

John Balliol's son. Edward was encouraged by the English to seize power from David II, but he never fully succeeded.

1346-1357
David is held prisoner in England. His nephew, Robert Stewart, rules Scotland as regent.

JANUARY 1356
Balliol finally abandons his claim to the Scottish throne.

OCTOBER 1357
After agreeing to pay a huge ransom for his release, David returns to Scotland.

1357-71
Childless, facing rebellions from his nobles, and unable to pay the English his ransom, David names Edward III as his successor. The Scottish Parliament refuses to recognize the deal.

FEBRUARY 1371
David dies and is succeeded by Robert Stewart, who becomes Robert II.

THE 'DANDY KING'

RICHARD II
1377–1399

Born: January 6, 1367

Crowned: Westminster,
June 22, 1377

Died: Pontefract Castle,
February 14, 1400

Richard II was ten when he
became King and a teenager
when he faced the
Peasants' Revolt.

In 1399, he was forced from
the throne by his cousin,
Henry Bolingbroke. He died,
a prisoner, a year later.

Edward III died in 1377. His son, the Black Prince, had died before him, so his ten-year-old grandson, Richard, came to the throne. People had high hopes for Richard but, because he was a child, a council of nobles ruled for him, led by his uncle, John of Gaunt.

At first, the council ruled well, but in 1381, the nobles introduced a very unpopular tax – the Poll Tax. Everyone had to pay the same, no matter how rich or poor they were. Riots broke out when officials tried to collect the tax, and this turned into an uprising known as the Peasants' Revolt.

The Peasants' Revolt

In Kent, a craftsman named Wat Tyler gathered a huge group of rebels and marched on London. Richard was just 14, but he kept his cool. He met the rebels and listened to their demands.

During the negotiations, the Lord Mayor of London killed Wat Tyler – but Richard still managed to persuade the rebels he was on their side, and they went home.

But, when the uprising was over, Richard went back on his promises. He rounded up the rebel leaders and had them executed.

Richard II was the first English king to commission a lifelike portrait of himself.

Made in the 1390s, this larger-than-life-size painting, which shows the King in his coronation robes, hangs in Westminster Abbey.

The Lords Appellant

Richard was a proud, temperamental young man. He believed God had chosen him to be King, and he didn't like being told what to do. In 1386, John of Gaunt left England, and Richard appointed a new ruling council, made up of his closest friends. Many nobles were very angry they'd been overlooked.

In 1387, a group of nobles in Parliament, known as the 'Lords Appellant', got rid of Richard's advisers, and appointed their own council. The King was furious, but the lords were so powerful there was little he could do at the time.

A vengeful king

Ten years later, Richard took his revenge. He claimed there was a plot against him, and executed or banished most of the Lords Appellant, including John of Gaunt's son, Henry Bolingbroke. Then, in 1399, Gaunt died. Richard confiscated his land, disinheriting Bolingbroke.

Henry the Usurper

Bolingbroke, who had been exiled to France, swiftly retaliated. He raised an invasion force, and took control of most of southern and eastern England.

Richard was captured and imprisoned in the Tower of London. Eventually he agreed to give up his crown, and Bolingbroke was proclaimed King Henry IV.

The deposed King was taken to Pontefract Castle where he starved to death. Henry claimed Richard refused to eat, but it's possible he was murdered.

A refined court

Richard II may have faced many challenges as King, but he also ruled over a court filled with luxury, art and culture.

Richard, sometimes referred to as the 'Dandy King', had a taste for fine clothes, and is said to have invented the handkerchief.

He wore a badge showing his emblem, the white stag, and gave similar badges to his friends.

A recipe book written by the King's chief cook includes all kinds of rich foods eaten at the royal court, such as blancmange, spiced goose, and even a recipe for porpoise broth.

Richard also supported the work of a number of poets in his court, including William Langland, John Gower and Geoffry Chaucer.

A divided family

In the 1450s a bitter civil war broke out between rival branches
of the Plantagenet family – the houses of Lancaster and York.
The two sides fought for the throne in what was later called the
Wars of the Roses, named after their family emblems.

EDWARD III
1327-1377

Edward
'the Black Prince'

John of Gaunt, Duke of Lancaster
m. (1) Blanche of Lancaster; (3) Katherine Swynford

Edmund,
Duke of York

RICHARD II
1377-1399

HENRY IV
1399-1413

John
Beaufort

Joan Beaufort
m. Ralph
Neville

Richard,
Earl of Cambridge

HENRY V
1413-1422

John
Beaufort, Earl
of Somerset

Richard
Neville

Richard, Duke of York
Acted as Protector in 1454-55

A white rose was the
family emblem of the
House of York.

HENRY VI
1422-61
& 1470-71

Margaret
Beaufort
m. Edmund
Tudor

Richard
Neville, Earl of
Warwick 'the
Kingmaker'

EDWARD IV
1461-70
& 1471-83

RICHARD III
1483-1485

George,
Duke of
Clarence

A red rose was the
family emblem of the
House of Lancaster.

HENRY VII   m. Elizabeth of York
1485-1509

EDWARD V
April-June, 1483

Richard,
Duke of York

Stewarts

Robert II was the first Stewart King of Scotland.
His dynasty took the name Stewart because his
father was High Steward of Scotland, a title
given to his ancestors by David I.

ROBERT THE BRUCE
1306-1329
m. (1) Isobel
(2) Elizabeth

Marjorie,
m, Walter,
High Steward of Scotland

DAVID II
1329-1371

ROBERT II
1371-1390
m. (1) Elizabeth
(2) Euphemia

David,
Earl of
Strathearn

Walter,
Earl of Atholl

+ 2
sisters

ROBERT III
1390-1406

Walter,
Earl of Fife

Robert,
Duke of Albany

Alexander,
Earl of Buchan

+ 5 sisters

David
died in 1402

JAMES I
1406-1437

+ 3 sisters

JAMES II
1437-1460

+ 6
sisters

JAMES III
1460-1488

Alexander,
Duke of Albany

David,
Earl of Moray

John,
Earl of Mar

STEWARTS, LANCASTER & YORK

The 15th century was a time of violent unrest and bloodshed. In England, Henry IV's seizure of the throne opened the way for a split in the royal family. This led to a 30-year civil war that would bring an end to the Plantagenet dynasty. Three out of five Scottish kings came to the throne as children. But, despite kidnappings, imprisonment, rebellions at home and wars with the English, the Stewarts managed to hold on to power.

In this portrait Henry IV is shown holding a red rose, the emblem of the House of Lancaster – his branch of the Plantagenet family.

"Uneasy lies the head that wears the crown."

This line is spoken by the king in Shakespeare's play, *Henry IV, Part Two.*

Having overthrown and murdered his cousin to become King, the real Henry IV was tormented with guilt, and with fear that the same would happen to him.

HENRY IV
1399–1413

Born: April 3, 1366, Bolingbroke Castle, Lincolnshire

Crowned: October 13, 1399

Died: March 20, 1413, Westminster

Henry deposed his cousin, Richard II, to become the first Lancastrian King of England. He himself faced challenges to his leadership and died of exhaustion.

THE UNEASY KING

Adventurous, ambitious and charming, the young Henry of Lancaster had always been a threat to his cousin, Richard II. Henry was the eldest son of the influential John of Gaunt, Duke of Lancaster, and was due to inherit a lot of land and power.

By 1397, Richard had come to suspect that Henry was plotting against him, so he banished him, and confiscated his inheritance. Henry was devastated. With the help of other disgruntled English nobles, he returned, imprisoned Richard, and made himself King.

But Henry wasn't the only claimant to the throne, and in the first few months of his reign, he had to put down many violent attempts to overthrow him. Meanwhile, Richard died in prison.

Rebellion in Wales

Then, in 1400, Henry faced a major rebellion in Wales. What started as a local feud between a marcher lord, Reginald de Grey, and a Welsh nobleman, Owain Glyndwr (pronounced Glendower), quickly escalated into a full-scale revolt against English rule. Many of Henry's English enemies saw this as an opportunity to overthrow the King, and joined with Glyndwr, too.

One of the English rebels was a skilled warrior, Henry Percy, nicknamed 'Hotspur'. He had been in charge of putting down the Welsh rebellion, until he switched sides. Henry IV took his army to fight Hotspur, and they clashed in a fierce battle at Shrewsbury in 1403. Hotspur was killed and Henry won the battle, but the Welsh revolt went on for years.

A guilty conscience

By 1409, Henry had finally defeated the rebels. But he couldn't be happy with what he had achieved. Suffering from poor health and racked with guilt about Richard II's death, Henry died in 1413, a broken man.

The Welsh Prince

Owain Glyndwr led a long-running revolt against Henry IV's rule in Wales.

In 1400, Welsh nobles declared him Prince of Wales, and in 1404, he had enough support to call his own parliament. He even plotted with English nobles to take over England itself.

But Glyndwr's rebellion fizzled out after 1409, and he was forced into hiding.

No one knows where or how he died, but he is still celebrated in Wales as a national hero.

This is Harlech Castle, in Wales. Owain Glyndwr made it his headquarters, and held his own parliamentary meetings there.

ROBERT II
1371–1390

Born: March 2, 1316

Crowned: Scone,
February 1371

Died: April 19, 1390

The grandson of Robert the
Bruce, Robert II had acted
as regent for David II before
becoming the first Stewart
King of Scotland. He spent
most of his reign fighting
rebellious nobles.

ROBERT III
1390–1406

Born: c.1337

Crowned: Scone,
August 14, 1390

Died: April 4, 1406

Disabled by a kick from a
horse in 1388, Robert III
was unfit to rule for much
of his reign.

JAMES I
1406–1437

Born: Dunfermline,
December 1394

Crowned: May 1424

Married: Joan Beaufort

Died: February 20, 1437

Kidnapped when he was 11,
James I was a prisoner of
Henry IV of England for 18
years until a ransom was paid
for his release.

THE HOUSE OF STEWART

In 1371, Robert Stewart inherited the Scottish throne. He was already an experienced ruler, having acted as regent for his younger uncle, David II, for many years before becoming king himself. As regent, he had led successful battles against the English, and held a strong influence over parliament and the Scottish nobles.

But, by the time David died, Robert was in his fifties and frail. As King, he retreated from public life, and left his sons to rule on his behalf. He died in 1390, leaving his eldest son, Robert, to succeed him.

Unruly brothers

Robert III was already 53 when he was crowned. Like his father, he suffered from ill health, and a lack of authority. He was unable to control his brother, Alexander, the Earl of Buchan, who was plundering towns in the north of Scotland, and many people thought that Robert was unfit to rule. Meanwhile, another of Robert's brothers, Robert, Duke of Albany, had captured and killed the King's son and heir, David, hoping to seize power.

"The worst of kings"

To try to save his remaining son, James, Robert sent him to France in 1406. But, James's ship was attacked by pirates on the way, and he was given over to Henry IV of England. Distraught, Robert died just days after hearing the news. Before his death he declared, "bury me in a dunghill and write, *Here lies the worst of kings and the most wretched of men.*"

The hostage king

Although he became King after his father's death, James I spent the first 18 years of his reign as a prisoner in England. He was well looked after and educated in the English court, and even married Joan Beaufort, a great-granddaughter of Edward III of England.

In 1424, James was released from captivity and returned to Scotland, where powerful nobles had taken control in his absence. The King immediately set about stamping his authority. He had his enemies executed, and set up a supreme court, putting anyone who disobeyed him on trial.

This proved to be James's downfall. His actions upset many Scottish nobles, and on February 20, 1437, he was assassinated by his uncle, Walter, Earl of Atholl.

A royal poet

James I was a cultured and intelligent monarch, who loved art and poetry.

He even wrote a long, semi-autobiographical poem, *The King's Quair* (quair means 'little book' in Old Scots).

The poem begins with a young man who can't sleep, so he decides to write a poem about his life.

The lonely poet gazes out of his prison window, sees a beautiful woman and falls in love with her.

He enters a trance-like sleep, and in his dreams, he visits three goddesses who offer to help him win his love.

As the poet wakes, a white dove brings him a scroll with a poem on it, telling him that he will have his desire and his love will set him free.

This portrait of James I was made around the time he was crowned, aged 30.

"We few, we happy few, we band of brothers; For he today who sheds his blood with me Shall be my brother..."

These aren't Henry's own words, but part of a rousing speech delivered by the King to his men before the Battle of Agincourt in Shakespeare's play, *Henry V*.

This 15th-century illustration shows the French and English armies at the Battle of Agincourt, October 1415 – a key battle of the Hundred Years' War.

HARRY OF ENGLAND

Henry V came to the throne ready for action. Made Prince of Wales at his father's coronation in 1399, Prince Harry, as he was known, gained his first military experience aged only 15 at the Battle of Shrewsbury.

The Prince gained political experience too, leading the King's Council when Henry IV's health began to fail. He was so successful that there was even talk of the King stepping down so his son could take over.

Once more unto the breach

In 1413, Henry IV died and Prince Harry, now 26, became Henry V. The new King was determined to renew the war that Edward III had begun against France, and to claim the French throne for himself.

HENRY V
1413-1422

Born: August 9, 1387

Crowned: April 9, 1413

Married: Catherine of France, June 1420

Died: Vincennes, France August 31, 1422

A great warrior, King Henry V renewed the Hundred Years' War with France, winning a major victory at the Battle of Agincourt. He died while on campaign in France.

Popular politics

But first, Henry needed to win the support of his nobles. He gave back lands and power to many of his father's old enemies, and he had the body of Richard II reburied at Westminster Abbey. With the nobles on his side, he had no trouble convincing Parliament to fund an invasion of France.

Taking France by storm

On August 11, 1415, Henry set sail for France with a force of 10,000 men. In September, they stormed the port city of Harfleur. Then, on October 25, they defeated a French army more than three times their size at the Battle of Agincourt. It was a triumphant victory, and in November, Henry and his men returned to London to a heroes' welcome.

Troyes

Henry went from strength to strength. In August 1417, he returned to France. By January 1419, he had conquered Normandy, and in May 1420, he made King Charles VI of France sign the Treaty of Troyes, recognizing Henry as his heir. To seal the deal, Henry married the French King's daughter.

Henry died two years later, just weeks before he would have been crowned in Paris. He left his son, Henry, as his heir.

This portrait of Henry V shows him as a thoughtful, almost monkish, ruler, but he was also a shrewd politician and a talented military tactician.

> ### Religious rebels
>
> In the 1380s, a religious teacher named John Wycliffe began to criticize the Church. He believed that people didn't need priests to teach them about religion, and made the first translation of the Bible from Latin to English.
>
> Wycliffe's followers became known as Lollards. They were seen as a threat to authority, and Henry V had many of them burned at the stake, including a former friend who had attempted to stage an uprising.

HENRY VI
1422-61
& 1470-71

Born: Windsor Castle,
December 6, 1421

Crowned King of England
twice: 1429 & 1470

Crowned King of
France: 1431

Married: Margaret of Anjou,
April 23, 1445

Died: murdered in the Tower
of London, May 21, 1471

Henry VI became King when he
was only nine months old, so his
uncles ruled in his place. From
the 1450s, he and his relatives
fought for power in
what became known
as the Wars of
the Roses.

THE WARS OF THE ROSES

Henry VI was only nine months old when he
inherited the English throne from his father.
Less than two months later, his grandfather, Charles VI
of France, died, and Henry became King of France too.

Family rivalries

Until Henry was old enough to rule in his own right,
his uncles acted as regents in England and France.
However, Charles VI's son, Charles VII, declared war
on England and proclaimed himself King of France.

The cost of the war added to growing friction
among the royal family, the English nobles and
Parliament, and the situation didn't improve when
Henry came of age.

This statue of Henry VI stands in the
courtyard of Eton College school.

He founded it in 1440, and King's
College, Cambridge,
in 1441, to give
free education to
scholars from
poor families.

King or pawn?

Henry was a gentle, religious man, but he wasn't a natural leader, and he didn't know how to control his nobles. Things went downhill in August 1453, when Henry suffered a bout of insanity. For the next 18 months, he was unfit to rule.

Richard, Duke of York was made Protector to govern in the King's place. But when Henry recovered, the Duke of York tried to stay in control.

A family at war

England was plunged into a bitter civil war – the Wars of the Roses. On one side, the Yorkists' emblem was a white rose. On the other side were the Lancastrians, so-called because Henry was descended from the Duke of Lancaster. Their emblem was a red rose.

Power flipped between the two sides in a series of bloody battles. At first, the Yorkists seemed to be winning. But in 1460 the Duke of York was killed. His head was cut off and displayed wearing a paper crown.

'Kingmaker'

The following year, the Yorkists came back fighting. Led by Richard Neville, the Earl of Warwick, they defeated Henry and crowned York's son Edward IV. Neville was nicknamed 'the Kingmaker' as a result, but when Edward fell out with him, Neville switched sides.

He drove Edward out, and in 1470 he put Henry back on the throne. But Edward returned the following spring. He defeated the Lancastrians, and threw Henry in the Tower of London, where he was murdered.

Losing France

The Hundred Years' War that had been running against France since the reign of Edward III continued under Henry VI.

At first, the English, with their skilled archers, had the upper hand.

Then, in 1429, the French armies were led to victory under the inspirational leadership of a peasant woman known as Joan of Arc, who claimed to hear voices from God. Later that year, Charles VII of France was crowned at Rheims.

In 1430, the English captured Joan, accused her of witchcraft and had her burned at the stake.

The following year, Henry was crowned King of France in Paris.

But by then the English were losing the war. When the fighting finally came to an end in 1453, Henry had lost all his French territories, except Calais.

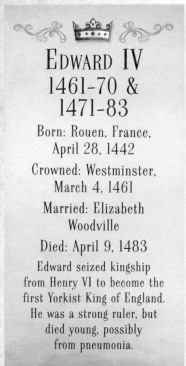

EDWARD IV
1461-70 &
1471-83

Born: Rouen, France,
April 28, 1442

Crowned: Westminster,
March 4, 1461

Married: Elizabeth
Woodville

Died: April 9, 1483

Edward seized kingship
from Henry VI to become the
first Yorkist King of England.
He was a strong ruler, but
died young, possibly
from pneumonia.

This is a portrait of Elizabeth
Woodville. She wasn't a
princess, but Edward married
her for love, which was very
rare for monarchs at that time.

THE HOUSE OF YORK

"The commoners love and adore him, as if he were their God," reported an observer at Edward IV's coronation in 1461. Popular, pleasure-loving and attractive, Edward of York became King aged 18, having already proved himself a brave and charismatic soldier general.

An unpopular match

For the first four years of Edward's reign, government was dominated by his powerful cousin, Richard Neville, 'the Kingmaker'. But, in 1464, the cousins fell out. Neville, who had been trying to arrange a marriage for Edward with a French princess, discovered that the King had married an English woman named Elizabeth Woodville behind his back.

The Woodvilles had fought for the Lancastrians. Now, the new Queen brought many of them with her to the Yorkist court, showering them with gifts and titles.

Not surprisingly, this angered many Yorkist nobles, especially Neville. Enraged, he joined forces with the Lancastrians. Then, in 1470, he deposed Edward and put Henry VI back on the throne.

Show of strength

Edward, his brother Richard, Duke of Gloucester, and a few faithful followers fled to Burgundy. They gathered an army and invaded England in March 1471. By May, the Lancastrians had finally been defeated. Neville, Henry VI and Henry VI's son were all dead, and Edward was King again.

Family matters

Back in power, Edward had his baby son crowned Prince of Wales, and gave many of Neville's lands to his loyal brother, the Duke of Gloucester. His other brother, George, Duke of Clarence, was more of a problem. During the wars, he had sided with Neville, hoping to become King himself. Clarence was thrown in the Tower and was later executed – supposedly drowned in a barrel of Malmsey wine.

Taking charge

After years of civil war, Edward IV's reign brought peace and order to England. He improved the justice system, helped to build up foreign trade, steered clear of costly wars and kept Parliament on his side by ruling without demanding extra taxes.

The King worked hard, but he also played hard. He had a great love of food, and became obese. Aged only 40, Edward died suddenly. The peace of his reign proved short-lived, as civil war soon flared up again.

The King's printer

In 1476, an English merchant named William Caxton set up Britain's first ever printing press, in Westminster. One of his first publications was *The Canterbury Tales* by Geoffrey Chaucer.

Before printing was invented, books had to be copied out by hand. Printed books were quicker and cheaper to produce in large numbers, so they became available to a much wider audience.

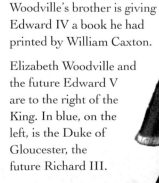

In this picture, Elizabeth Woodville's brother is giving Edward IV a book he had printed by William Caxton.

Elizabeth Woodville and the future Edward V are to the right of the King. In blue, on the left, is the Duke of Gloucester, the future Richard III.

JAMES II
1437–1460

Born: October 16, 1430

Crowned: Holyrood Abbey, March 26, 1437

Died: Roxborough Castle, August 3, 1460

James I's son became King when he was six, and his early years were dominated by power struggles between rival nobles. He was killed, during a siege, by an exploding cannon.

MINORITY KINGS

Only six years old when his father was murdered, James II of Scotland came to the throne amid civil unrest. His minority (the years before he was old enough to rule for himself) was dominated by bloody power struggles, as noble families, particularly the Douglases, fought to control the King and his court.

Dinner dates with death

In 1440, the King's advisers invited the 6th Earl of Douglas and his brother to a dinner at Edinburgh Castle. Lured to the castle, the Douglases were then dragged from the dinner table and beheaded.

Despite this, by the time James came of age, the Douglases had taken over many top government posts. In 1452, suspicious that they were plotting against him, James invited the 9th Earl of Douglas to dine with him at Stirling Castle, where he stabbed him. War broke out, and it was three years before James finally defeated the Douglases.

Capturing the castle

In August 1460, James laid siege to Roxborough Castle. It was one of the last Scottish castles still in English hands after the Wars of Independence, and James wanted it back. But disaster struck. One of the King's own cannons exploded and killed him.

This painting is the only authentic portrait there is of James II. He was nicknamed 'Fiery Face' because he had a red birthmark on his left cheek.

History repeats itself

James's nine-year-old son was crowned James III. Once again, Scotland had a minor on the throne, and ambitious noble families vying for control.

In 1469, James took power for himself. But he made himself unpopular with his nobles by making peace with England. He also argued with his brothers, Alexander, Duke of Albany and John, Earl of Mar, and had them arrested. Mar died mysteriously in prison.

Invasion and rebellion

Albany escaped, returning in 1482 with an English invasion, led by Edward IV's brother, Richard. James was imprisoned, and Albany briefly took charge.

James was restored to power in 1483, but he did nothing to improve relations with his nobles. In 1488, they rose against him. James was defeated at the Battle of Sauchieburn and died soon after.

Stirling Castle was the site of many dramatic events in Scottish history.

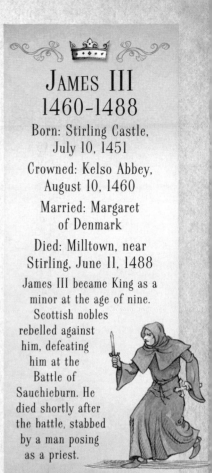

JAMES III
1460-1488

Born: Stirling Castle, July 10, 1451

Crowned: Kelso Abbey, August 10, 1460

Married: Margaret of Denmark

Died: Milltown, near Stirling, June 11, 1488

James III became King as a minor at the age of nine. Scottish nobles rebelled against him, defeating him at the Battle of Sauchieburn. He died shortly after the battle, stabbed by a man posing as a priest.

EDWARD V
April–June 1483

Born: November 4, 1470

Crowned: Never

Died: September 1483?

Deposed by his uncle,
imprisoned and probably
murdered in the Tower.

RICHARD III
1483–1485

Born: October 2, 1452

Crowned: July 6, 1483

Died: Killed at the
Battle of Bosworth,
August 22, 1485

The last Yorkist King of
England. Probably responsible
for his nephew
Edward V's
murder.

TREASON! TREASON!

Edward V was 12 years old when he became King, in April 1483. So his uncle Richard was named as Protector, to rule until he was old enough to take over for himself.

However, the young King's mother, Elizabeth Woodville, and her family had other ideas. As soon as they heard the news of Edward IV's death, they set up their own regency council, determined to take power for themselves. But Richard found out what the Woodvilles were up to, and intercepted them on the way to London.

The Princes in the Tower

Edward was then escorted to the royal apartments at the Tower of London, where his younger brother, Richard, later joined him.

On June 25, Parliament ruled that Edward IV's marriage to Elizabeth Woodville had been illegal and their sons were illegitimate. Richard was proclaimed King, and crowned 10 days later.

For a while, people reported seeing the princes playing in the gardens of the Tower. But, after September that year, they were never seen again.

Richard III was considered tall and handsome
for his times, but the Tudors portrayed him
as evil and deformed. They claimed he
had a crooked back to match what they
saw as a crooked nature, but there's no
evidence to support this.

The Battle of Bosworth

Just three months after his coronation, one of Richard's former allies staged a rebellion. It was crushed, but a more serious threat was looming in the shape of Henry Tudor, the last remaining Lancastrian heir.

On August 22, 1485, on a marshy field near Leicester, Richard and Henry Tudor battled it out. Richard, wearing a thin, gold crown over his helmet, led a cavalry charge and fought his way through Henry's bodyguards. At that point, Sir William Stanley, who was there in support of the King, ordered his troops to switch sides. Richard was hacked down, crying, "Treason! Treason!"

Legend has it that Richard's crown was found under a bush, and used to 'crown' Henry Tudor right there on the bloodstained battlefield.

Making history

After 30 years of fighting, the Wars of the Roses was finally over. Richard was the last of the Plantagenet kings, and the last King of England to die in battle.

Richard III's reign had lasted just two years and two months, but the true fate of the Princes in the Tower remains a mystery to this day. They were probably killed on Richard's orders, though others, including Henry Tudor, also stood to benefit from their deaths.

It is often said that history is written by the winners. The new King, Henry Tudor, launched a smear campaign against Richard, and Shakespeare went on to portray him as a monstrous villain. What he was really like, and whether he was guilty, we may never know.

Enduring mystery

This painting of the Princes in the Tower was made by the 19th-century artist Sir John Everett Millais. Very little is known about them or what they looked like.

In 1674, the bones of two children were unearthed during building work at the Tower. Many believed these were the princes' remains, and Charles II had them buried in Westminster Abbey.

Scientists have since examined the skeletons and have been unable to prove their identity.

Uniting the crowns

In 1503, Henry VII's daughter, Margaret, married James IV of Scotland, bringing the English and Scottish royal families together. When Elizabeth I died without an heir, James VI of Scotland became James I of England, uniting the two countries under a single monarch.

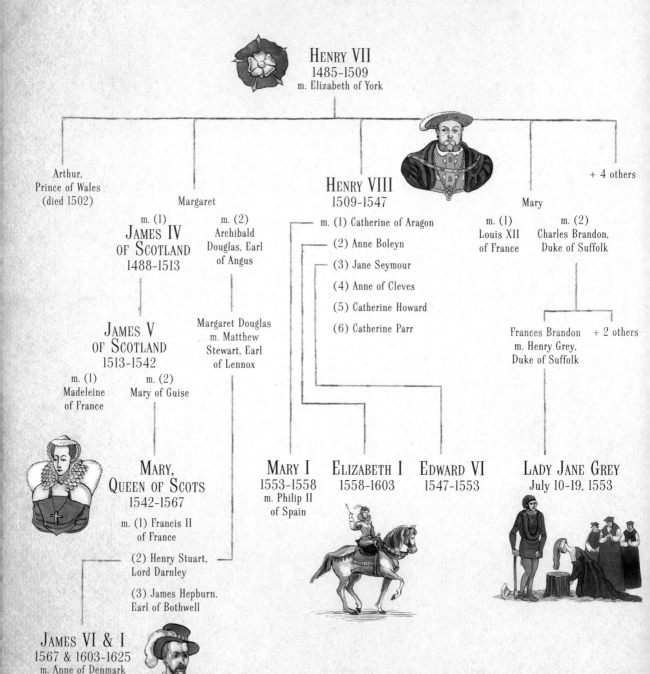

HENRY VII
1485–1509
m. Elizabeth of York

Arthur,
Prince of Wales
(died 1502)

Margaret

HENRY VIII
1509–1547

+ 4 others

Mary

m. (1)
**JAMES IV
OF SCOTLAND**
1488–1513

m. (2)
Archibald
Douglas, Earl
of Angus

m. (1) Catherine of Aragon

(2) Anne Boleyn

(3) Jane Seymour

(4) Anne of Cleves

(5) Catherine Howard

(6) Catherine Parr

m. (1)
Louis XII
of France

m. (2)
Charles Brandon,
Duke of Suffolk

**JAMES V
OF SCOTLAND**
1513–1542

Margaret Douglas
m. Matthew
Stewart, Earl
of Lennox

Frances Brandon
m. Henry Grey,
Duke of Suffolk

+ 2 others

m. (1)
Madeleine
of France

m. (2)
Mary of Guise

**MARY,
QUEEN OF SCOTS**
1542–1567

m. (1) Francis II
of France

(2) Henry Stuart,
Lord Darnley

(3) James Hepburn,
Earl of Bothwell

MARY I
1553–1558
m. Philip II
of Spain

ELIZABETH I
1558–1603

EDWARD VI
1547–1553

LADY JANE GREY
July 10–19, 1553

JAMES VI & I
1567 & 1603–1625
m. Anne of Denmark

THE TUDORS & STEWARTS

In 1485, Henry Tudor defeated Richard III at
the Battle of Bosworth, and became the first
Tudor King of England. His descendants were
some of the most famous and influential
monarchs in British history.

The Scottish royal family, the Stewarts, had
a troubled relationship with the Tudors.
But, through the marriage of James IV to
Margaret Tudor, the Scots would eventually
inherit the English throne.

"The best
businessman to
sit on the English
throne."

Sir Winston Churchill's
view of Henry VII

This is a portrait of Henry VII.
The flowers in the golden arch
above his head are red roses,
the symbol of his family, the
Lancasters.

HENRY VII
1485-1509

Born: January 28, 1457

Crowned: Westminster
Abbey, October 30, 1487

Married: Elizabeth of York

Died: April 21, 1509

Seized the throne from
Richard III, ending the Wars
of the Roses, and becoming
the first Tudor monarch.
Created the Tudor Rose, the
emblem of the Tudor dynasty.

THE FIRST TUDOR

Henry VII didn't have a very strong claim to the throne, but he didn't let that stand in his way. He came to power after defeating Richard III in battle and winning the Wars of the Roses.

A rosy romance

The Wars of the Roses had raged for 30 years between two branches of the royal family: York and Lancaster. Henry was a Lancastrian but, shortly after he was crowned, he married Edward IV's daughter, Elizabeth of York. Their marriage united the warring houses, and strengthened Henry's claim to the throne.

Getting down to business

When Henry VII first came to power, the royal finances were in a terrible state. Henry completely turned this around. He raised money by imposing huge taxes on his nobles, and he worked hard to strengthen ties with other countries, encouraging foreign trade and avoiding expensive wars. He made a peace deal with France, married his son Arthur to the Spanish Princess Catherine of Aragon, and his daughter Margaret to James IV of Scotland.

Keeping the crown

Having seized the throne himself, Henry had to fight off other claimants. In 1487, a boy named Lambert Simnel posed as Richard III's nephew (on his wife's side) and demanded to be made King. He was even crowned in Ireland before he was found out.

Then, in 1491, a man named Perkin Warbeck claimed he was Edward V's brother. James IV of Scotland helped him invade England, but the plan failed. Warbeck was defeated and executed for treason.

Three funerals

Henry's son and heir, Prince Arthur, died in 1502, aged just 16. Henry was devastated – he'd had high hopes for Arthur. Another blow came in 1506, when Henry's wife Elizabeth died. The King was so heartbroken that he withdrew from public life.

Henry died in 1509. He'd ruled the country so well that his second son, Henry, succeeded him without opposition.

The Tudor rose

To celebrate his marriage to Elizabeth of York, Henry VII created a new family emblem. It was made up of his family symbol, the red rose of Lancaster, and Elizabeth's, the white rose of York. Henry called it the Tudor Rose.

Queen of Hearts

The picture of the Queen in some packs of playing cards is based on a portrait of Henry VII's wife, Elizabeth. If you look closely, you can see she's holding the white rose of York.

JAMES IV
1488-1513

Born: March 17, 1473

Crowned: Scone, June 24, 1488

Married: Margaret Tudor

Died: September 9, 1513

Supported the arts and sciences, and helped set up the first printing press in Scotland. Made peace with Henry VII, but died fighting Henry VIII's army at the Battle of Flodden.

James IV, shown in this portrait, was intelligent and charismatic, but also suffered from serious depression.

The royal scientist

James was fascinated by science, and tried out all sorts of experiments himself.

He sent two babies to live with a woman who couldn't speak, to see if they would make up their own language. But they never learned to speak at all.

James founded the Royal College of Surgeons in Edinburgh, and even tried his hand at dentistry.

A RENAISSANCE KING

James IV came to the Scottish throne after his father, James III, was killed fighting rebels at the Battle of Sauchieburn. After he was crowned, he discovered that the rebels had adopted him as their figurehead. He felt so guilty about the role he'd unwittingly played in his father's death that he wore a heavy iron belt for a month every year as a form of penitence. Every year, he added extra links to make the chain heavier.

Despite the violent start to his reign, James became one of the most successful and popular kings Scotland ever had.

He was a strong and fair ruler, and he was determined to establish Scotland as a thriving independent nation.

90

An age of progress

James ruled Scotland during the Renaissance – a time of great cultural change in Europe. Scientists and artists were coming up with radical new ideas, and the King embraced their discoveries.

James helped set up the first printing press in Scotland, and founded universities. He built a Scottish navy to rival England's, and commissioned the *Great Michael* – the largest wooden ship ever made.

War and peace

At first, James was very hostile to the English King, Henry VII. He even got involved in a failed attempt to overthrow him. But, over time, relations improved, and in 1502 they signed the Treaty of Perpetual Peace, to put an end to all fighting. As part of the deal, James IV married Henry's daughter, Margaret Tudor. It was through this marriage that a Scottish king, James VI, would eventually inherit the English throne.

Divided loyalties

Anglo-Scottish relations went downhill when Henry VIII became King of England, and invaded France. James was torn between the peace treaty he'd signed with England, and an older treaty with France. He sided with the French, and invaded England.

It was a disastrous decision. His army was defeated at the Battle of Flodden on September 9, 1513. James himself was killed, and his bloodied coat was sent to Henry VIII as proof.

James's child bride

The English Princess Margaret Tudor was only 14 when she married 30-year-old James, and at first she was very homesick.

After James died, Margaret married again. Two of her grandchildren – Mary, Queen of Scots, and her cousin Lord Darnley – became husband and wife.

Fatal Flodden

The Scots outnumbered the English at the Battle of Flodden, but English troops crushed them, and thousands of Scottish soldiers died. Every noble family in Scotland is said to have lost a man in the battle.

BLUFF KING HAL

HENRY VIII
1509-1547

Born: June 28, 1491

Crowned: Westminster
Abbey, June 24, 1509

Married: six times

Died: January 28, 1547

Famous for his six wives, and
for breaking with the Catholic
Church and founding the
Church of England.

Henry VIII was a man of extremes. He ate and drank so much that he made himself ill, and he spent most of the money his father had saved throwing lavish banquets and tournaments. He was charming, but very temperamental – and it could be deadly to cross him.

The young king

Henry came to the throne as a slim, handsome 18-year-old. He loved wrestling and playing tennis, and he was extremely well-educated – he spoke several languages, and was a brilliant musician. But signs of his ruthlessness were apparent from the start.

As soon as he became King, he had two of his father's advisers, who'd been widely disliked, executed on false charges – just to make himself more popular.

An ambitious adviser

Henry's chief adviser was a clever, charming man named Thomas Wolsey, who encouraged Henry to attack France, to try to take over French land. In 1513, England beat France at the Battle of the Spurs. Wolsey secured a peace deal afterwards, and negotiated a marriage between Henry's sister, Mary, and King Louis XII of France.

This imposing portrait of Henry was
painted by Hans Holbein the Younger.

The 'other king'

Wolsey and Henry became close friends. Wolsey became so powerful that he was known as *alter rex*, which means 'other king' in Latin. He was made both a Cardinal (an important churchman) and Lord Chancellor (the most important minister in England), so he had enormous influence over both the Church and the government.

Wolsey lived in great luxury, and built himself several fabulous palaces, including Hampton Court. But he worked hard, too. One of his greatest achievements was arranging a peace summit between Henry VIII and Francis I of France. It was held in 1520 in northen France, and became known as the 'Field of the Cloth of Gold'.

This painting shows Henry at the 'Field of the Cloth of Gold'. Fountains flowed with wine, and golden tents were dotted about, giving the event its name.

Wrestling kings

Henry VIII and Francis I of France were old enemies. But when they met for a peace summit in France, known as the 'Field of the Cloth of Gold', they got on really well. They visited each other's tents for late-night chats, and even held a wrestling contest.

"Had I served God as carefully as I served my King, he would not have deserted me in my old age."

The last words of Thomas Wolsey, Henry's adviser, who was accused of treason.

Monks and monasteries

After Henry broke away from the Catholic Church, he closed down all the English monasteries.

In October 1536, 30,000 people, including monks, marched on Lincoln to protest. This was known as the Pilgrimage of Grace. Henry arrested their leaders and had them executed.

Heirless Henry

Henry married his brother's widow, Catherine of Aragon, and in 1516, she gave birth to a daughter, Mary. But Henry desperately wanted a son to succeed him. This became known at court as the King's 'Great Matter.'

Then Henry fell in love with Anne Boleyn, one of Catherine's ladies-in-waiting. Henry decided he wanted to divorce Catherine and marry Anne. The trouble was, England was a Catholic country. Divorce had to be agreed by the Pope, but the Pope wouldn't allow it. Wolsey tried to change the Pope's mind, but the Pope stood firm. Henry was furious with Wolsey for failing to secure him a divorce, and accused him of treason – but Wolsey died before his trial took place.

The Church of England

Henry wracked his brains for a solution to his problem. It was Anne herself who provided it. She gave him a book, banned by the Church, by a controversial scholar named William Tyndale. It said that a true Christian Prince should govern the Church as well as the State. This appealed to Henry's ego, and he decided to make himself the Head of the Church in England, so he could grant himself a divorce.

In 1534 he made Parliament pass the Act of Supremacy, declaring Henry 'the only supreme head on Earth of the Church in England.' The Church of England was born.

Henry forced the clergy to acknowledge him as the Head of the Church. Anyone who refused risked being executed.

Unlucky Anne

At first, Henry was devoted to Anne, his new wife. She was already pregnant when the couple married, and Henry believed a male heir would soon be born. But on September 7, 1533, Anne gave birth to a red-haired baby girl – Elizabeth.

Over the next two years, Anne miscarried several times, and Henry began to think she would never give him a son. He accused Anne of having affairs with a string of men, even though she was innocent. Henry had her executed for treason on May 19, 1536.

Witchy whispers

Anne was unpopular at court, where people spread gossip that she was a witch.

A son at last

The day after Anne's execution, Henry proposed to Jane Seymour, who had been a lady-in-waiting to both his previous wives. They were married ten days later. On October 12, 1537, Jane Seymour gave birth to a boy, Edward.

Henry finally had the son he'd longed for. But happiness at Edward's arrival was overshadowed by grief when Jane died, 12 days after giving birth. Henry was devastated. He wore black for three months, and didn't remarry for three years.

This is Henry VIII's second wife, Anne Boleyn. She wasn't considered very beautiful, but when Henry met her, he became infatuated with her.

A bad match

In 1540, Henry decided it was time to find another wife. His Chancellor, Thomas Cromwell, advised him to marry a German noblewoman named Anne of Cleves. Henry sent the artist Holbein to paint Anne, so he could see what she looked like. He liked Holbein's portrait (left), so a marriage contract was agreed.

But when Henry met Anne in the flesh, he thought she was ugly. They were married, but they divorced after six months. Henry beheaded Cromwell for arranging such an unsuitable marriage.

Richly rewarded

When Henry decided to divorce Anne of Cleves, she didn't complain. Henry was so grateful that he gave her several houses and a generous allowance.

She became known as 'the King's beloved sister', and they remained friends for the rest of their lives.

Henry's fifth wife

Just days after Henry divorced Anne, he married 19-year-old Catherine Howard. Henry was 30 years older than his new, young wife, and she wasn't attracted to him at all. She had an affair with a courtier named Thomas Culpepper. When Henry found out, he had her executed.

When Wolsey fell from grace, Henry VIII took Hampton Court for himself. It became one of his best-loved palaces.

A third Catherine

In 1543, Henry married a rich widow named Catherine Parr. The marriage was a fairly happy one. She persuaded Henry to get to know his daughters, who had both been sent away from court when their mothers fell from grace.

In 1546, some of Henry's officials turned against Catherine, and tried to convince Henry to arrest her for arguing with him about religion. But Catherine persuaded Henry she'd only argued with him to distract him from the pain caused by an ulcer in his leg.

Old King Henry

By the end of his life, Henry was unwell and bad-tempered. He'd injured his leg in a jousting accident and became so fat he couldn't walk. He died, aged 55, on January 28, 1547, and he was buried in St. George's Chapel, Windsor Castle, next to his beloved third wife, Jane Seymour.

A rhyme to remember

Here's a rhyme to help you remember the order of Henry's wives, and what happened to them:

Divorced

Catherine of Aragon

Beheaded

Anne Boleyn

Died

Jane Seymour

Divorced

Anne of Cleves

Beheaded

Catherine Howard

Survived

Catherine Parr

This is a portrait of James V with his second wife, Mary of Guise.

Henry VIII had tried to prevent their marriage by proposing to Mary himself, but she refused – he'd already executed one of his wives, and she was scared he'd execute her too.

JAMES V
1513–1542

Born: April 10, 1512

Crowned: Stirling Castle, September 21, 1513

Married: Madeleine of France (d. 1537) and Mary of Guise

Died: December 14, 1542

'King of the Commons' who didn't trust nobles. Married two French noblewomen.

Angered his uncle, Henry VIII, by refusing to break with the Catholic Church. Fought Henry's army at the Battle of Solway Moss and suffered a terrible defeat.

FAITHFUL TO FRANCE

James V came to the Scottish throne in 1513, after his father, James IV, died in the Battle of Flodden. The new King was only 17 months old, so his mother, Margaret Tudor, ruled the country for him. When she got married again, to Archibald Douglas, Earl of Angus, James's uncle, James Stewart, Duke of Albany, seized power and took over as regent.

Kidnapped!

But Margaret and Douglas's marriage deteriorated, and Margaret began to side with James Stewart over her husband. Douglas was furious. In 1525, he kidnapped James and held him hostage, hoping to gain power and influence over the young King.

But it didn't work. In 1528, James managed to escape. He was now 14, and he finally started to rule for himself. The first thing he did as King was to send Douglas and his family into exile and seize their lands.

98

French affairs

James wanted to reinforce the long-standing ties between Scotland and France – often referred to as the 'Auld Alliance'. So, in 1537, he married Madeleine, the daughter of the King of France. But, just seven weeks after arriving in Edinburgh, she died.

A year later, James married Mary of Guise, the daughter of a French duke. His marriage strengthened his relationship with France, but damaged his ties with England. James's uncle, Henry VIII, had wanted James to marry his daughter Mary. By choosing his French allegiances over his English ones, James made his temperamental uncle very angry.

The final straw

James V and Henry VIII also clashed over religion. England had broken away from the Catholic Church, and Henry wanted Scotland to do the same. But James, a strict Catholic, refused.

Henry asked James to meet him in York, but James didn't turn up. Henry was so furious, he invaded Scotland. The two sides fought at Solway Moss on November 24, 1542, and the Scots suffered a terrible defeat.

James took the news of the defeat very badly, and he fell ill with a fever. About a week later, he heard that his wife had given birth to a baby girl – Mary. He was very upset not to have a male heir, as he didn't believe a woman could rule Scotland. The King died six days later, believing the Stewart dynasty was over.

The commoner King

James was nicknamed 'King of the Commons' because he liked riding around Scotland disguised as a farmer, so that he could spend time with ordinary people.

Not the last lass

When James heard his wife had given birth to a girl, Mary, he said the Stewart dynasty, "cam wi' a lass, and it'll gang wi' a lass" ("started with a girl, and it will end with a girl"). The crown had come to his family through Robert the Bruce's daughter, Marjorie, and he believed his family would stop ruling Scotland after Mary died.

But he was proved wrong. Mary's son, James VI, became King, and he and his descendants went on to rule England as well as Scotland.

This portrait was painted when Edward was about a year old.

A BOY KING

When Henry VIII's long-awaited son Edward was born, people all over England rejoiced. But it wasn't long before he became King. Henry died in 1547, and Edward came to the throne, aged nine.

A new kind of Christianity

Henry VIII had split from the Catholic Church in 1534 so he could grant himself a divorce – not because he objected to Catholicism itself. But, in Europe, some people had begun to see the Catholic Church as corrupt, and had broken away too. They introduced ideas and reforms, which became the basis for a new form of Christianity: Protestantism.

This soon spread to Britain, and Edward was the first English monarch to be brought up as a Protestant.

EDWARD VI
1547–1553

Born: October 12, 1537

Crowned: Westminster Abbey, February 20, 1547

Died: July 6, 1553

Long-awaited son of Henry VIII, the first English monarch to be raised as a Protestant. The Church was dramatically reformed during his reign. Died from tuberculosis aged just 15.

Edward's reformation

Because Edward was a child, England was ruled by the King's Council of nobles. Along with Thomas Cranmer, Archbishop of Canterbury, they brought in radical Church reforms to make England a truly Protestant country.

Stained glass windows were destroyed, altars were turned into tables, and services were held in English instead of Latin for the first time. Cranmer introduced a Protestant prayer book, which everyone had to use.

But, in 1553, Edward developed tuberculosis. He was just 15, but it was clear he didn't have long to live.

THE NINE DAYS' QUEEN

Edward's Catholic half-sister, Mary Tudor, was next in line to the throne. Cranmer and the leader of the King's Council, John Dudley, knew she would overturn their religious reforms if she became Queen. So they persuaded Edward to name his cousin Lady Jane Grey – who was also Dudley's daughter-in-law – as his successor. Edward died on July 6, 1553, and Jane was declared Queen.

Mary takes control

But many people were furious that Jane had been chosen over Mary, who had a much better claim to the throne. Mary gathered support, and marched on London to take power. At this point, Jane's supporters, and even her father, deserted her. Once in control, Mary charged Jane with treason. She pleaded guilty, and was executed in February 1554. She had been Queen for only nine days.

This painting of Lady Jane Grey's execution was made in the 19th century by a French artist, Paul Delaroche.

LADY JANE GREY
July 10–19, 1553

Born: 1537

Ascended to throne: July 10, 1553

Crowned: never

Married: Lord Guildford Dudley

Executed: February 12, 1554

Protestant cousin of Edward VI, named as his heir in an attempt to stop his Catholic half-sister Mary from ruling the country. Declared Queen, but was deposed after nine days, and executed.

Weeping for Jane

In 1834, when French artist Paul Delaroche's painting (left) of Lady Jane Grey's execution was first exhibited in Paris, many people who went to see it were so moved that they wept.

MARY I
1553-1558

Born: February 18, 1516

Crowned: Westminster
Abbey, July 19, 1553

Married: Philip II of Spain

Died: November 17, 1558

The first Queen of England
to rule in her own right.
Mary was a Catholic, and
made England a Catholic
country once more. She was
nicknamed 'Bloody Mary' for
killing Protestants.

This portrait of Mary was
painted after her engagement
to Philip II of Spain.

Mary, Mary,
quite contrary,
How does your
garden grow?
With silver bells,
and cockle shells,
And pretty maids
all in a row.

Many people think this
nursery rhyme is
about Mary I.

BLOODY MARY

Mary I was the first Queen of England to rule in her own right, rather than being married to a king. She came to the throne on a wave of public support. Most people felt that, as Henry VIII's eldest surviving child, she was the rightful Queen.

But during her five-year reign, Mary, who was a strict Catholic, made herself unpopular by trying to impose Catholicism on England.

Falling for Philip

Mary was 37 when she came to the throne. Soon after becoming Queen, she decided to find a husband. She wanted a child so her Protestant half-sister Elizabeth wouldn't become Queen after her.

Mary's cousin, the Catholic Charles V of Spain, suggested she marry his son, Philip. Mary met Philip for the first time on July 23, 1554, and they were married two days later.

The Wyatt rebellion

Mary's marriage to Philip was extremely unpopular, especially when England got dragged into a war on Spain's behalf. This sparked an uprising. A rebel named Thomas Wyatt managed to gather a force of about 4,000 men. They marched on London, demanding that Elizabeth be crowned. But the rebellion was crushed. Wyatt was executed, and Elizabeth imprisoned, even though she'd had nothing to do with the plot.

Reforming the reforms

Mary was determined to make England a Catholic country again. She had nearly 300 Protestants burned at the stake for refusing to convert to Catholicism, including Archbishop Cranmer. This earned her the nickname 'Bloody Mary'.

Mary died aged 42. She never had a child, so Elizabeth became Queen – and England became Protestant again.

Picture perfect

Before Mary met her future husband, Philip, she saw a portrait of him painted by Titian, a famous Italian artist.

As soon as Mary looked at the portrait, she declared she was in love with Philip.

Martyrs' memorials

Many Protestants were burned at the stake on Mary's orders. They became known as martyrs.

Monuments were built in their memory all over the country, such as this Victorian memorial in Oxford, built close to the place where Archbishop Cranmer was killed.

ELIZABETH I
1558-1603

Born: September 7, 1533

Crowned: Westminster Abbey, January 15, 1559

Married: Never

Died: March 24, 1603

Known as the 'Virgin Queen' because she never married. Remembered as one of the most successful of all English monarchs. Ruled during a 'golden age' of art and culture.

"Beggar woman and single, far better than Queen and married."

Elizabeth I, 1563

Pricey parties

Elizabeth often visited nobles in different parts of her kingdom, and she expected them to give her a luxurious place to stay. They went to great lengths to please her. Some even converted their houses into the shape of an 'E'.

GOOD QUEEN BESS

Elizabeth I's life was difficult from the start. She was only three years old when her father had her mother executed. When she became Queen, she faced opposition from people who thought women were weak and shouldn't be rulers.

But Elizabeth proved once and for all that women could rule just as well as men – if not better – and became one of the best-loved and most successful monarchs in history.

Married to her country

From the beginning of her reign, Elizabeth proved to be an excellent politician. She encouraged foreign trade and exploration, and gained control over government finances.

At first, everyone wondered who the Queen would marry, but she refused to choose a husband. She knew that whoever she picked, she risked offending others – and she didn't want to share her power with anyone. Because she never married, Elizabeth became known as the 'Virgin Queen'.

A balancing act

Under Elizabeth, England once again became a Protestant country, although she was tolerant of Catholics. This all changed, however, when Elizabeth discovered some Catholics were plotting against her – including her own cousin, Mary, Queen of Scots.

Keeping up appearances

Elizabeth knew it was important to project an image of
herself as a strong monarch. She made sure paintings
made her look majestic and powerful.

Elizabeth's coronation portrait shows off her
white skin, long hair and delicate hands.

Here, Elizabeth is shown standing on a map of Britain,
to show her command of her kingdom. She seems to
command the elements too: the sun shines before her,
and dark stormy days are behind her.

Elizabeth was 69 when this was painted, but
artists never showed her looking old. Here
she's shown holding a rainbow of peace.

Elizabeth made sure there were
no unflattering pictures of
her. She chose certain
artists to paint official
portraits. Others could
copy them – but only
if they had a license.

MARY, QUEEN OF SCOTS

Mary, Queen of Scots grew up in the French court. She was married to Francis II of France, and changed the spelling of her name from 'Stewart' to the French style 'Stuart'. But in June 1560, Mary's mother, Mary of Guise, died. In Mary's absence, she'd been ruling Scotland – which was in the grip of a civil war. In December, Mary's husband died too. Mary left France and went to Scotland to claim her throne.

Marriage and murder

In 1565, Mary married her cousin, Lord Darnley. But it soon became clear that he was violent and jealous, and it was a very unhappy marriage. In 1567, Darnley was found dead at a house in Edinburgh. He'd been strangled, and the house had been destroyed by an explosion.

Just four months later, Mary married James Hepburn, the Earl of Bothwell, the man suspected of murdering Darnley. Mary was unpopular with her people – she was Catholic and most Scots were Protestant – and this was the final straw. There was an uprising against her, and in 1568 she fled the country.

Mary was very beautiful, and she was 6ft (1.8m) tall, which made her look very impressive.

Seeking refuge

Mary hoped her cousin, Elizabeth I, would protect her. But many Catholics thought Mary should be Queen of England, and Elizabeth suspected Mary of plotting against her – not without good reason.

Elizabeth arrested Mary, who spent the next 19 years imprisoned in different castles and houses around England.

This is Mary's prayer book, and the rosary she carried to her execution.

In 1585, Elizabeth's head spy, Francis Walsingham, uncovered a plot to assassinate Elizabeth and place Mary on the throne. It was clear Mary was a major threat, and couldn't be allowed to live.

Although Elizabeth signed the death warrant, she didn't want to execute her cousin, and kept delaying the execution. After Mary was finally beheaded, Elizabeth claimed it had been carried out without her permission, and she threw the man responsible into the Tower of London.

Witness to an execution

On February 7, 1587, Mary was executed at Fotheringay Castle. She spent the last hours of her life praying and writing letters.

According to one witness, the executioner asked Mary's forgiveness, and she replied: "I forgive you with all my heart."

A faithful pet

Mary was very fond of her pet dog. She even took it with her to her execution, hiding it under her skirts.

Afterwards, it refused to leave its mistress's body. The story goes that Mary's ladies-in-waiting took the dog away, but it wouldn't eat, and died of a broken heart.

This portrait was painted to celebrate the defeat of the Spanish Armada.

Behind Elizabeth on the left, you can see the Spanish ships approaching England. Behind her on the right, the ships are being destroyed in a storm.

"I know I have the body of a weak and feeble woman; but I have the heart of a King, and a King of England, too."

Part of Elizabeth's rousing speech to the English forces, to inspire them to fight hard against the Spaniards.

THE SPANISH ARMADA

Almost immediately after Mary was executed, Elizabeth faced another threat – this time from Philip II of Spain. English seamen had been attacking and looting Spanish ships in the Caribbean. Philip was furious, and sent a huge fleet of ships (*armada* in Spanish) to attack England.

But when the Armada set sail in July 1588, a fleet of English ships was waiting off the coast of northern France. The English set fire to eight of their own boats and sent them crashing into the Spanish fleet. After several battles, many Spanish ships were destroyed, and most of the rest were wrecked in a storm. Not one English ship was lost. Elizabeth gave a triumphant speech to cheering crowds in London, thanking God for the victory.

Leicester, a lost love

Just after the defeat of the Armada, Elizabeth was devastated by the death of one of her closest friends, Robert Dudley, Earl of Leicester. They'd known each other since they were children, and they'd had a romance even though Dudley was married.

In 1560, Dudley's wife had died after falling down some stairs. Elizabeth seriously considered marrying him, but her advisers strongly disapproved of the match. She and Dudley remained close, however, and when he remarried, Elizabeth was very upset.

An insolent Earl

After Dudley died, Elizabeth grew fond of his stepson, Robert Devereux, Earl of Essex. She was 34 years older than him, but he flattered her, and she gave him important military jobs.

In 1599, she sent Essex to Ireland to crush a rebellion against English rule. The campaign was such a disaster that Elizabeth put Essex under house arrest. After he was released, he plotted to overthrow the Queen. He failed, and was executed in 1601.

The end of an era

Elizabeth died at Richmond Palace on March 24, 1603. Her coffin was carried down the Thames to Whitehall. Crowds of stunned mourners gathered in Westminster to watch her funeral procession pass by – many of them had never known another monarch. Their ageless, all-powerful Queen had died. Was England's 'golden age' all over?

A golden age

Elizabeth's reign was seen as a golden age for English literature.

Elizabethan poets and playwrights included Edmund Spenser, Christopher Marlowe and, most famous of all, William Shakespeare. He wrote plays such as *Romeo and Juliet* which were performed at London playhouses and at court.

Famous flatterers

Among the explorers whose company Elizabeth enjoyed were Sir Francis Drake, the first Englishman to sail all the way around the world, and Sir Walter Raleigh, an explorer who brought the American plants tobacco and potatoes to England.

Uniting the kingdoms

This family tree shows how the Stuart King James IV of Scotland came
to inherit the English throne from the Tudors as James I of England.

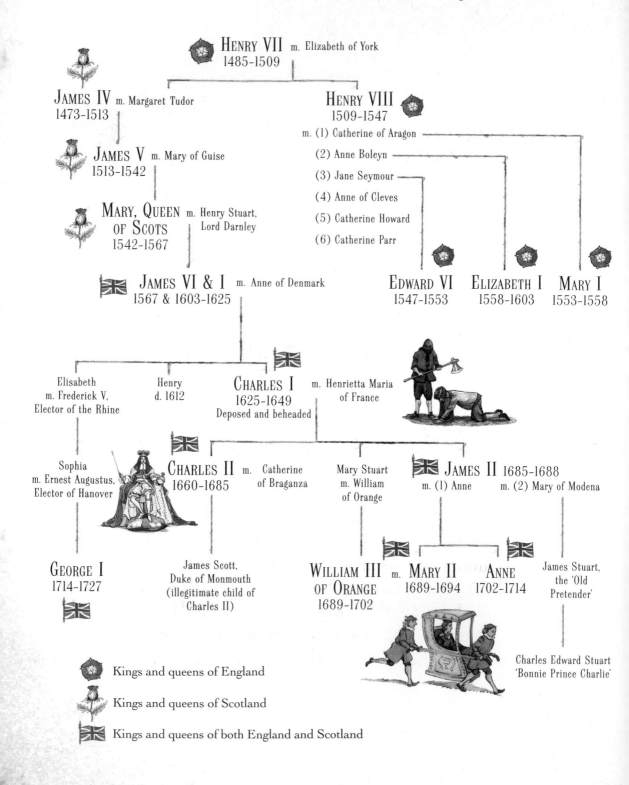

HENRY VII m. Elizabeth of York
1485-1509

JAMES IV m. Margaret Tudor
1473-1513

HENRY VIII
1509-1547

m. (1) Catherine of Aragon

(2) Anne Boleyn

(3) Jane Seymour

(4) Anne of Cleves

(5) Catherine Howard

(6) Catherine Parr

JAMES V m. Mary of Guise
1513-1542

MARY, QUEEN m. Henry Stuart,
OF SCOTS   Lord Darnley
1542-1567

EDWARD VI
1547-1553

ELIZABETH I
1558-1603

MARY I
1553-1558

JAMES VI & I m. Anne of Denmark
1567 & 1603-1625

Elisabeth
m. Frederick V,
Elector of the Rhine

Henry
d. 1612

CHARLES I   m. Henrietta Maria
1625-1649   of France
Deposed and beheaded

Sophia
m. Ernest Augustus,
Elector of Hanover

CHARLES II m. Catherine
1660-1685   of Braganza

Mary Stuart
m. William
of Orange

JAMES II 1685-1688

m. (1) Anne   m. (2) Mary of Modena

GEORGE I
1714-1727

James Scott,
Duke of Monmouth
(illegitimate child of
Charles II)

WILLIAM III m. MARY II
OF ORANGE   1689-1694
1689-1702

ANNE
1702-1714

James Stuart,
the 'Old
Pretender'

Charles Edward Stuart
'Bonnie Prince Charlie'

Kings and queens of England

Kings and queens of Scotland

Kings and queens of both England and Scotland

The
STUARTS

In 1603, Queen Elizabeth I of England died
and was succeeded by James VI of Scotland.
For the first time, the two nations were
united under one monarch.

Parliament grew more and more powerful
under the Stuarts, and in 1641 a civil war
broke out between Charles I and Parliament.
In 1649, the King was deposed and
executed, and the monarchy was abolished.
Charles II was restored to the throne, but the
balance of power was changed forever.

JAMES VI & I

1567 &
1603-1625

Born: Edinburgh, 1566

Crowned King of Scots:
Stirling Castle,
July 29, 1567

Crowned King of England:
Westminster Abbey,
July 25, 1603

Died: March 27, 1625

Extravagant King of England
and Scotland who frequently
argued with Members
of Parliament.

Flagged up

James still ruled England
and Scotland as separate
nations, with their own
churches and parliaments.
What he really wanted was
a united Great Britain, but
Members of Parliament
rejected this idea.

He did, however, create
a new British flag that
combined the English and
Scottish flags.

English
flag

British
flag

Scottish
flag

THE WISEST FOOL

Just minutes after Queen Elizabeth died, a horseman raced to Edinburgh with a message for the Scottish King, James VI. He was to be James I of England. Elizabeth died childless, and James – as son of Mary Queen of Scots, Elizabeth's cousin – was next in line to inherit the throne. He was the first Stuart King of England.

Difficult youth

James had been crowned King of Scots at just 13 months old, after his father was murdered and his mother was forced from the throne.

When he was 16, he was kidnapped by conspirators hoping to overthrow him and, throughout his childhood, many of his regents were killed. In later life, he was convinced he would be stabbed, so he took to wearing protective padded clothing at all times.

Man of culture

Despite his turbulent upbringing, James always found time for education and the arts. He loved fine art and commissioned portraits by fashionable Dutch painters, such as Anthony Van Dyck. He ordered a new translation of the Bible and wrote books and pamphlets on a wide range of subjects, including witchcraft and one of the earliest arguments against smoking tobacco.

The King also encouraged scientific research – even testing out the first ever submarine. James prided himself on his knowledge, calling himself the "great schoolmaster of the land".

Religious issues

James's Protestant upbringing made Catholics suspicious of him. One group, including a man named Guido (Guy) Fawkes, even planned to blow up Parliament with James inside. Luckily, James was warned about the plot, and the conspirators were caught and executed.

Some Protestants weren't happy with the King, either. James kept a close circle of courtiers who he loved spoiling with expensive gifts. His lavish ways offended a group of strict Protestants, known as Puritans, who believed in a simple, hard-working life. In 1620, 102 Puritans sailed to North America where they could live and worship as they chose. They became known as the Pilgrim Fathers.

The Gunpowder Plot

At midnight on Fifth of November, 1605, soldiers found Guy Fawkes in the vaults under the Houses of Parliament, next to barrels of gunpowder. Fawkes was arrested and executed.

This day is still celebrated in Britain today, with bonfires and fireworks.

Problems with Parliament

James was described by a politician at the time as the "wisest fool in Christendom". Despite his education, he didn't always deal with his subjects very tactfully, and found it difficult to get along with Parliament.

He believed in the 'divine right of kings' – the idea that a king was chosen by God and shouldn't be questioned. When Members of Parliament disagreed with his decisions, he argued with them, or simply dissolved Parliament and ruled without them. By the time he died, his disputes with Parliament had made him unpopular.

James spent thousands of pounds a year on clothes. In this portrait, painted in 1619, he's showing off some of his finery.

This portrait of Charles I is by Van Dyck. The pose was intended to make Charles look tall and kingly, when in fact he was a small, shy man.

Charles had many grand portraits painted of himself, often high up on a horse, looking down on his subjects. Because of this, he is sometimes described as the 'Cavalier King'.

CHARLES I
1625-1649

Born: Dunfermline, Scotland, 1600

Married: Henrietta Maria of France, 1625

Crowned: Westminster Abbey, February 2, 1626

Executed: January 30, 1649

A shy but stubborn man with refined tastes in the arts, Charles made many mistakes as King. His strong beliefs led to a civil war that ended with him being beheaded.

THE CAVALIER KING

James I's second son, Charles, was a weak and sickly child who stammered when he spoke, and idolized his popular, sporty older brother, Henry. But Henry died aged 18, and Charles was suddenly thrust into the limelight. He was now next in line to the throne.

Searching for respect

When Charles became King, he was determined to leave the shadow of his brother and his father. While James had tried to avoid conflict, Charles soon entered into wars in Europe. Instead of marrying a Protestant, Charles chose a Catholic princess, Henrietta Maria of France, as his Queen. This made many MPs worry that Charles wanted to make England Catholic again.

Catholic tastes

Like his father, Charles was a believer in the 'divine right of kings', and he upset Members of Parliament by repeatedly ignoring their advice. He also appointed his friend, William Laud, as Archbishop of Canterbury. Laud was Protestant but liked grand, Catholic-style church services – and enforced them across England. This turned Puritans and even moderate Protestants against Charles.

Ruling alone

The wars in Europe were expensive, so Charles asked Parliament for money. Its members refused to help him. Charles was furious and decided he could do better alone. In 1629, he disbanded Parliament. For 11 years, he governed the country and raised taxes on his own.

Then, in 1637, Charles made a big mistake. He tried to introduce Laud's services and a new prayer book in Scotland. But most Scots were Presbyterians with similar beliefs to Puritans, so this didn't go down well.

King in crisis

Riots broke out all over Scotland, with people vowing to go to war. Reluctantly, Charles had to recall Parliament to ask for money to raise an army. This was the chance Charles's rivals had been waiting for. They arrested Laud and another of his allies. Then, a group of MPs, led by a Puritan named John Pym, drew up a set of laws that drastically reduced the King's powers. Charles had no choice but to accept.

Royal pastimes

Charles was an educated man with lots of hobbies. His main passion was fine art, and he spent thousands of pounds building up a huge collection of paintings.

He made a Dutch artist, Anthony Van Dyck, his court painter.

Charles and Henrietta Maria loved performing in masques – a type of play with music, dancing, singing and acting.

Charles was also a keen chess and tennis player.

Civil War battles

This map shows where the major battles of the Civil War took place and when.

The symbols show which side came out on top each time.

Preston, 1648

Marston Moor, 1644

Naseby, 1645

Edgehill, 1642

Oxford ●

London ●

⬛ Won by Parliament

♛ Won by Royalists

This scene shows a re-enactment of a battle from the Civil War. The foot soldiers are fighting with pointed wooden pikes.

CIVIL WAR

In January 1642, Charles stormed into the House of Commons with a plan to arrest Pym and the other troublemakers. He was sure he'd still have the support of the majority of MPs. He was wrong. Pym and his group had already escaped, and the King's act of aggression turned even neutral MPs against him.

Charles left London and headed north to gather an army. Meanwhile, his opponents, the people who supported Parliament, also prepared for war.

Bloody battles

With a small, but loyal, Royalist army, Charles declared war in August 1642. For the next seven years, there was violent fighting, and thousands of people died. The Parliamentarians had the upper hand. Their general, Oliver Cromwell, raised a highly-trained 'New Model Army' of skilled and disciplined men. Compared to the King's men, Cromwell's soldiers were fierce, tough and frightening. At the Battle of Naseby in 1645, they crushed the Royalist troops.

Playing games

Left without an army, Charles gave himself up to the Scots, hoping they'd protect him. But, in 1647, they handed him over to the Parliamentarians.

Still, Charles refused to give up. Pretending to negotiate with Cromwell, he also made secret deals with the Scots, persuading them to join him against Cromwell's men. This turned out to be a disaster. Charles and the Scots lost the Battle of Preston, and in August 1648, he was arrested and taken to London.

Death of a king

The New Model Army was determined to get rid of Charles, so they put him on trial for treason. The King was found guilty and sentenced to death.

On January 30, 1649, Charles I was beheaded outside the Banqueting House in London. A crowd gathered to watch, many horrified to see a king being killed. Instead of cheering as he died, they groaned. For the first time in a thousand years, the country had no monarch. Who would rule instead?

Charles on trial

Throughout his trial, Charles refused to plead. He said that no court had the right to try a king, and laughed at the charges against him.

The day of Charles's execution was freezing cold. Not wanting to shiver and appear scared, Charles asked for an extra shirt to wear.

When Charles arrived at his place of execution, no one wanted to be the executioner. Finally, a hooded man stepped forward. His identity is still a mystery today.

A SERIOUS MAN

With Charles I dead, Parliament declared that the monarchy was abolished. Oliver Cromwell, the straight-talking, God-fearing MP, was now in charge of England. He had risen quickly through the ranks of the Parliamentarian army, and he was now the most powerful man in the country.

"Warts and all"

When Oliver Cromwell became Lord Protector, he asked to be painted "warts and all" – not flatteringly like Charles I.

For the first 30 years of his life, Oliver Cromwell made a living from farming the modest amount of land he owned in Cambridgeshire.

It wasn't until he was elected MP for Huntingdon in 1628 that he started to clash with Charles I in Parliament.

As a Puritan, Cromwell was a fierce opponent of the extravagant and wasteful lifestyle of Charles I.

Problem Royalists

Cromwell didn't hesitate to get rid of all traces of Charles I and any Royalist supporters that might still be a threat. Taking his New Model Army to Ireland, Cromwell ordered the killing of thousands of Royalist supporters there.

Meanwhile, the Scots had crowned Charles I's son, also named Charles, King of Scots. Charles had fled to France during the Civil War but had now returned to lead an army against Cromwell. Cromwell again acted quickly, and crushed Charles and his troops at the Battle of Worcester in 1651.

Plain-clothed leader

His opponents defeated, Cromwell changed his battle gear for plain, black clothes to address his first Parliament. He gave himself the title of Lord Protector, and set out his ideas for reforming England. But, like Charles I, Cromwell found it difficult to get on with his Parliament. When MPs disagreed with him, he insulted them, then dismissed them.

Living in New Model England

While he allowed most people to worship as they pleased, Cromwell also believed that everyone should live by the same Puritan values as he did. He sent his army to enforce this throughout England. Cromwell's rule came to be known as the Commonwealth.

Inns and playhouses were shut.

People were fined for taking part in activities such as playing sports.

Christmas and Easter were banned, and replaced with days of fasting (going without food) instead.

Women had to wear plain, dark dresses and cover their hair in public.

Churches were stripped of all decoration.

What happened during Charles II's reign?

1661 – Charles orders Oliver Cromwell to be dug up and his head cut off – to 'punish' him for Charles I's execution.

1665 – a deadly disease, the Bubonic Plague, hits London. 68,000 people die.

1666 – September 2, the Great Fire of London spreads across the city, raging for four days.

1669 – Sir Christopher Wren re-designs St. Paul's Cathedral, destroyed in the fire.

THE MERRY MONARCH

When Oliver Cromwell died in 1658, his son, Richard, took over. But he was unable to control either the army or Parliament, and resigned just a year later. Without a leader, there was soon the threat of another civil war. People began to wonder whether getting rid of the monarchy had been such a good idea.

The Restoration

Meanwhile, Charles Stuart had been living in exile in Europe for the last nine years. After his defeat at Worcester, he had spent 40 days trying to escape from England without being captured by Cromwell's search parties. He even spent a day hiding in an oak tree.

Charles was desperate to regain his birthright. He wrote to Parliament explaining how he could make England stable again. MPs saw his letter as a lifeline. They invited him back to England to be King Charles II.

A fun return

On May 29, 1660, Charles entered London to cheering crowds showering him with flowers. After dull, Puritan England, it was clear that times had changed. The monarchy was restored.

A fun-loving king, Charles was nicknamed the 'Merry Monarch'. He quickly re-opened the playhouses and inns that Cromwell had shut, and enjoyed horse racing, sailing and extravagant clothes. He also had a keen interest in science and architecture. He set up the Royal Society to promote scientific research, and commissioned architects to design elaborate buildings.

No heir?

Charles had an eye for the ladies, and fathered 14 illegitimate children with various mistresses, but none of them could be his heir. Sadly, he didn't have any children with his wife, a Portuguese princess, Catherine of Braganza. So, the next in line to the throne was Charles's brother, James.

Catholic suspicions

In the beginning, Charles wanted a good relationship with Parliament. But, he soon started to argue with MPs about religion. His brother, James, had converted to Catholicism and many MPs feared Charles was a Catholic, too. In a secret agreement, Charles promised Louis XIV of France that, in exchange for money, he would become a Catholic and help France in a war against the Dutch. When this story reached Parliament, MPs felt they couldn't trust Charles.

This picture shows Charles on the day of his coronation. He is riding on a white horse, wearing a tall hat and golden cloak.

CHARLES II
1660-1685

Born: London, 1630

Crowned: as King of Scots, Scone, January 1, 1651; as Charles II of England, Westminster Abbey, April 23, 1661

Died: February 6, 1685

Charming, pleasure-seeking king who encouraged the arts to flourish, but couldn't get on with Parliament.

JAMES II & VII
1685-1688

Born: 1633

Crowned: Westminster
Abbey, April 23, 1685

Deposed: December, 1688

Died: St. Germain-en-Laye,
France, September 16, 1701

Catholic King who clashed
with Parliament over religion.
He was finally forced from the
throne by William of Orange,
and spent the rest of his life
in exile in France.

Taking sides

In Charles II's time, there
were no political parties.
An MP had no allegiances,
other than to the people of
his borough, who elected
him to represent them.

James's succession divided
MPs. Those who supported
James became known as
Tories, and those against him
were called Whigs.

THE EXILED KING

As Charles II grew old, many Members of Parliament became concerned about the prospect of James, as a Catholic, succeeding him. To ensure England remained Protestant, they tried to make it illegal for a Catholic to become King. Charles defended James and argued against the proposal, dissolving Parliament four times. In 1681, he dismissed MPs for the final time, and ruled without them until his death.

An army man

Despite MPs' protests, James was crowned King. At 52, he had already lived an action-packed life. Imprisoned with his father during the Civil War, James had escaped and fled to France. While in exile, he joined the French, then the Spanish army, proving himself to be a skilled officer. Then, when Charles II became King, James was made commander of the Royal Navy. He was a man who was used to giving orders and having people obey him.

Devoted Catholic

As King, James attended Catholic church services and married a Catholic, Mary of Modena. But, he assured Parliament that he wanted England to remain Protestant. Although many MPs were suspicious of James's faith, they tolerated him. He was old, and had not been able to produce a male heir. They hoped that Princess Mary, his Protestant daughter from his previous marriage, would soon be Queen.

Rebellion

In July 1685, James faced his first challenge. The
Duke of Monmouth – an illegitimate son of Charles II,
and a Protestant – led an army to overthrow James.
The King's army easily defeated Monmouth and
his troops. Monmonth was captured, tried and
executed, along with 300 of his supporters.
Another 800 were sent away to be slaves. Many
people thought that this punishment was overly
harsh, and the trial became known as the
'Bloody Assizes'.

James decides

After the Monmouth uprising, James
was worried that Protestants might again
try to overthrow him. So, he replaced
prominent Protestant figures, such as
judges and army commanders, with Catholics
who might be more on his side. In 1687, he also issued
a declaration to abolish laws against Catholics – and
ordered this to be read out in church. When bishops
protested, he had them arrested. This made him even
more unpopular with the majority of Protestant MPs.

James II was tall and
handsome. This portrait was
painted when he had just
become King.

Catholic heir

In 1688, Mary of Modena gave birth to a son. Now
there was a Catholic heir to succeed James, his
Protestant opponents were horrified. In June, a group
of seven Whigs wrote to William of Orange, the
Protestant Dutch Prince, and husband of Princess
Mary. They invited him to invade and depose James.

Is it really yours?

When the Queen gave
birth to a son, some people
didn't believe he was really
James's. She had already
had 10 babies, but they had
all died. Gossip spread that
the baby had been smuggled
into the Queen's
bedroom in a
warming pan.

WILLIAM III & MARY II
1689–1702

Crowned: as joint monarchs, Westminster Abbey, April 11, 1689

William born: 1650

William died: March 8, 1702

Mary born: 1662

Mary died: December 28, 1694

The only King and Queen to rule jointly, William and Mary's reign ended with Parliament having more power than ever before.

This painting by J.M.W. Turner, shows William of Orange and his fleet advancing to England. The fact it was made in 1852, almost 200 years after the event, shows how significant it was.

A DUTCH INVASION

William of Orange readily accepted the challenge to overthrow his uncle, James II. He had been at war with France, a Catholic country, for years. He wanted the strong English navy, and the nation's wealth, at his disposal. He was also worried that if the English turned Catholic, they might ally with France against him. But publicly, he claimed he had come to England to "rescue the religion and the nation."

Glorious Revolution

On November 5, 1688, when England was celebrating the execution of Guy Fawkes over 80 years earlier, William landed at Torbay, in Devon, with 15,000 men. He then marched on London, gathering support along the way.

To James's surprise, many people he thought were his friends and supporters turned against him and joined sides with William. The King panicked. In December, he fled to France, terrified that he would be executed, like his father. William and Mary were crowned King and Queen in a coup known as the Glorious Revolution.

Mismatched couple

As a foreigner with an abrupt manner, William found it hard to endear himself to the public. He was often overseas fighting wars against the French, making clear what his motives for invading England had been. Mary, as a pretty, English girl, was much more popular. She was devoted to her husband and let him make all the decisions about running the country.

James returns

In 1689, James II, who still had support from Irish and Scottish Catholics, made a final attempt to regain his crown. He landed in Ireland with an army, planning to seize land from Protestant settlers there. But, at the Battle of the Boyne in July 1690, James's men were soon beaten by William's better organized troops. James again fled to France, where he stayed for the rest of his life. To avoid any more rebellions, in 1692, William made Catholic clans (families) in Scotland sign an oath of loyalty to him.

Bill of Rights

Unlike previous kings and queens who had tried, but failed, to get along with Parliament, William and Mary readily accepted the reforms MPs put forward. As soon as they were crowned, they accepted a Bill of Rights that limited the power of the monarchy. The Bill stated that monarchs weren't allowed to raise taxes or an army without the consent of Parliament, which had to be called at least every three years. It also declared that all future monarchs had to be Protestants.

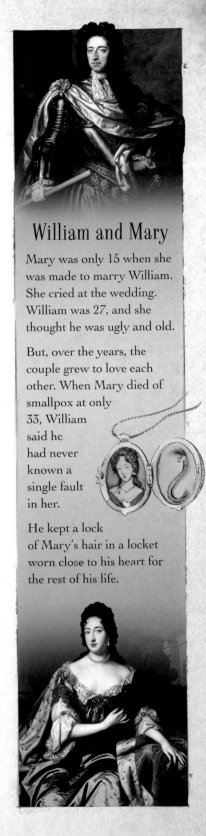

William and Mary

Mary was only 15 when she was made to marry William. She cried at the wedding. William was 27, and she thought he was ugly and old.

But, over the years, the couple grew to love each other. When Mary died of smallpox at only 33, William said he had never known a single fault in her.

He kept a lock of Mary's hair in a locket worn close to his heart for the rest of his life.

THE LAST STUART

In 1701, Parliament passed the Act of Settlement, which banned any Catholic, or anyone married to a Catholic, from becoming king or queen. This meant that Sophia of Hanover and her successors were the next in line after the Stuarts. Just a year later, William III fell off his horse while out hunting, and died of a lung infection. William and Mary had not had any children, which meant that Anne, Mary's Protestant sister, would now be Queen.

An English queen

Anne wanted to distance herself from William, the unpopular Dutchman. Wearing a bright red robe, Anne said clearly and confidently to her first Parliament, "I know my heart to be entirely English." Many people welcomed an English queen back on the throne. She soon entered into wars against France and Spain, where England won victory after victory. This made Anne even more popular.

Illness and tragedy

Anne rarely appeared in public. She suffered from gout – a painful swelling of the joints – and was in agony most of the time. It was often hard for her to walk. Anne was also frequently pregnant, giving birth to 19 children.

This portrait of Queen Anne was painted at the beginning of her reign. She was already 37 when she came to power.

Great Britain

Sadly, none of Anne's children survived. As she grew older, it was clear that she would not produce an heir. Many MPs in London started to worry about who would succeed her. Scotland still had its own Parliament, and not all of its members had accepted the Act of Settlement.

Anne's Catholic half-brother, James Stuart, was still living in exile in France and politicians worried that the Scots might try to crown him when Anne died. To prevent this, the English Parliament passed the Act of Union in 1707, uniting England and Wales with Scotland under one Parliament as Great Britain.

A new era

When Anne died in 1714, Stuart rule came to an end. Her closest Protestant relative was a German prince, named George. He was the son of Princess Sophia of Hanover and a great-grandson of James I. He would now become George I of Great Britain and Ireland.

Firm friends

Anne's best friend was Sarah Churchill. Anne felt so close to her friend, that she insisted Sarah call her "Mrs. Morley" to show that they were equals.

However, both Anne and Sarah were very opinionated. The two women argued so much that they eventually fell out, and Anne banished her from public life.

From Stuarts to Hanoverians

This family tree shows how George I was related to Anne. In 1707, the Act of Succession promised the throne to the Hanoverians. At the time there were 57 Stuarts with better hereditary claims to the throne, but they were all Catholic.

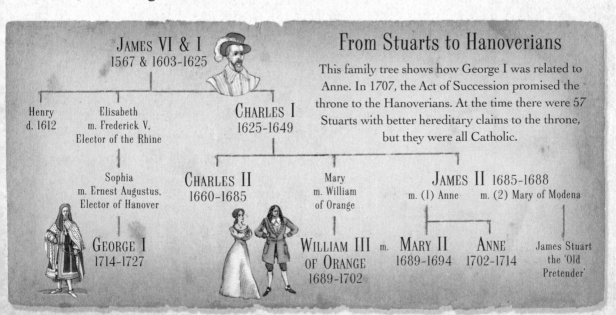

JAMES VI & I
1567 & 1603-1625

Henry
d. 1612

Elisabeth
m. Frederick V,
Elector of the Rhine

CHARLES I
1625-1649

Sophia
m. Ernest Augustus,
Elector of Hanover

CHARLES II
1660-1685

Mary
m. William
of Orange

JAMES II 1685-1688
m. (1) Anne   m. (2) Mary of Modena

GEORGE I
1714-1727

WILLIAM III m.
OF ORANGE
1689-1702

MARY II
1689-1694

ANNE
1702-1714

James Stuart
the 'Old
Pretender'

The House of Hanover

The Hanoverians got their name from the German state of Hanover, which they ruled along with Britain until 1837. Then, Victoria became Queen, but Hanover had to be ruled by a man, so it passed to her uncle, Ernest Augustus, instead.

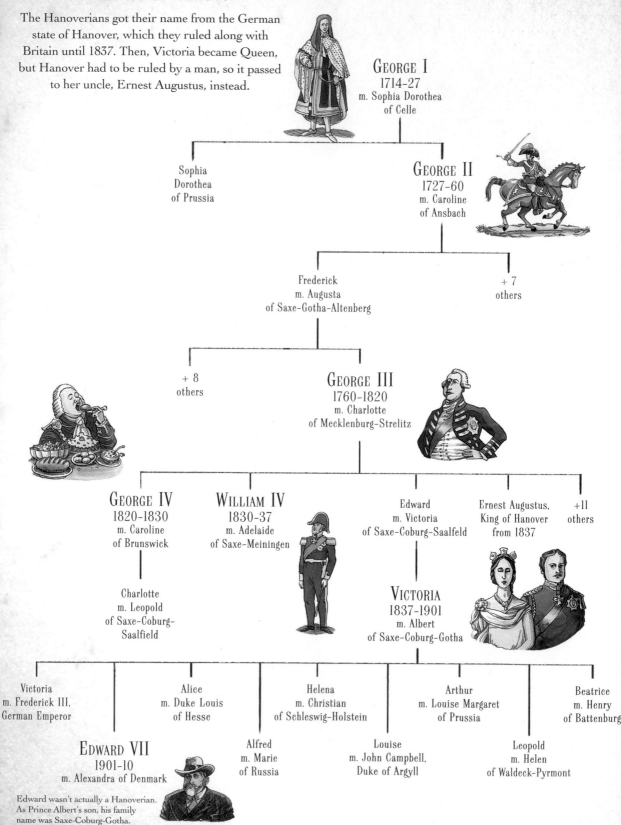

GEORGE I
1714-27
m. Sophia Dorothea
of Celle

Sophia
Dorothea
of Prussia

GEORGE II
1727-60
m. Caroline
of Ansbach

Frederick
m. Augusta
of Saxe-Gotha-Altenberg

+ 7
others

+ 8
others

GEORGE III
1760-1820
m. Charlotte
of Mecklenburg-Strelitz

GEORGE IV
1820-1830
m. Caroline
of Brunswick

WILLIAM IV
1830-37
m. Adelaide
of Saxe-Meiningen

Edward
m. Victoria
of Saxe-Coburg-Saalfeld

Ernest Augustus,
King of Hanover
from 1837

+11
others

Charlotte
m. Leopold
of Saxe-Coburg-
Saalfield

VICTORIA
1837-1901
m. Albert
of Saxe-Coburg-Gotha

Victoria
m. Frederick III,
German Emperor

Alice
m. Duke Louis
of Hesse

Helena
m. Christian
of Schleswig-Holstein

Arthur
m. Louise Margaret
of Prussia

Beatrice
m. Henry
of Battenburg

EDWARD VII
1901-10
m. Alexandra of Denmark

Alfred
m. Marie
of Russia

Louise
m. John Campbell,
Duke of Argyll

Leopold
m. Helen
of Waldeck-Pyrmont

Edward wasn't actually a Hanoverian.
As Prince Albert's son, his family
name was Saxe-Coburg-Gotha.

THE
HANOVERIANS

In 1701, Parliament passed the Act of
Settlement, making the ruler of Hanover the
heir to the British throne. George I became
King, not because he was next in line, but
because Parliament offered him the job.

Under the Hanoverians, life in Britain was
transformed by new industries and a growing
empire. The role of the monarchy changed too,
becoming increasingly symbolic. Real power of
government was now with Parliament.

GEORGE I
1714–1727

Born: May 28, 1660 at
Osnabrück, Hanover

Married: Sophia Dorothea
of Celle, 1682
(divorced 1694)

Crowned: October 20, 1714

Died: June 11, 1727

The first Hanoverian King of
Great Britain. He also ruled
the German state of Hanover.

This painting shows King
George and some friends
being rowed along the
River Thames.

George Frederick Handel, a
famous composer, is in red,
presenting his musicians to
the King. They are playing
his new composition,
Water Music.

GEORGE OF HANOVER

In 1714, George I arrived in Britain for the first time
to be crowned the nation's King. Although George
was James I's great-grandson, he didn't know much
about the country, and barely even spoke English.

Already 54 years old and set in his ways, George
desperately missed his homeland of Hanover, the small
German state that he ruled. He brought over as many
of his Hanoverian friends and servants as he could,
and took every chance to travel back.

Unhappy families

One person George was happy to leave behind was his
wife, Sophia. He was notorious for having affairs, but
in 1694 he had Sophia locked up after she had an affair
herself. She was a prisoner for the rest of her life, and
wasn't allowed to see their children. His
son, later George II, never
forgave him.

Ridicule and revolt

The reluctant King soon became a laughing stock to his new subjects, who thought he was dull and unsophisticated. Many nobles owned estates that were much bigger than Hanover, so didn't think George deserved much respect.

More seriously, many Catholics, particularly in Scotland, believed Queen Anne's Catholic half-brother, James Stuart, was her rightful heir. (Turn to page 127 to see James's family tree).

In late 1715, James's supporters, known as the Jacobites, staged an uprising, and James himself came over from France to lead them. But government troops soon defeated the Jacobite forces, and James fled back into exile.

This picture of George I was painted soon after he became King. It shows him dressed in a splendid set of robes.

Power behind the throne

By the time George became King, the power of government was already shifting from the monarch to Parliament. And because George knew little about British politics and wasn't interested in running the country, more and more control fell to his ministers. Soon the leading minister of the time, Robert Walpole, became the first Prime Minister.

Peaceful times

George was never popular, but his ministers kept the country running so smoothly that there was little for the British public to complain about. By the time he died, most people in Britain had accepted their new royal family.

The Maypole

George had many mistresses. One, Melusine von der Schulenberg, was so tall and thin that the British cruelly nicknamed her 'the Maypole'.

After George died, she kept a raven that she believed had the dead King's soul.

131

GEORGE II
1727–1760

Born: November 10, 1683,
Herrenhausen, Hanover

Married: Caroline of
Ansbach,
September 2, 1705

Crowned:
October 11, 1727

Died: October 25, 1760

George II was the second
Hanoverian King. He was the
last King of Britain to lead
his army into battle.

In this painting, George II
is shown overlooking the
battlefield at the Battle of
Dettingen.

His younger son, William
the Duke of Cumberland,
is by his side. William
was a respected military
commander, and was the son
George loved the most.

THE LAST SOLDIER KING

George I was succeeded by his son, George. Like his father, the new King was more German than British. Born and raised in Hanover, he spoke English with a heavy accent. But he embraced his new English life with a willingness that his father had never shown, proudly claiming that there was, "not a drop of blood" in his veins that, "was not British".

Boyhood and battlefields

George had always been fascinated by military history. As a boy, he memorized everything from battle dates to tactics and weaponry, and in 1708 he proved himself on the battlefield while fighting against France.

Even when he became King, he didn't give up his military career. In 1743, he became the last ever British monarch to lead an army into battle, winning against the French at the Battle of Dettingen.

Friend and adviser

George was lucky to have a strong wife, Caroline of Ansbach. They'd met in June 1705, and the young George was instantly besotted. They married within months.

Although Caroline and George weren't much alike, their union was long and affectionate. George indulged her passion for philosophy and the arts, while she laughed off the many affairs he had – she knew that he was devoted to her despite his string of mistresses.

Highly intelligent, Caroline was also George's most trusted adviser. She was a skilled politician, and helped him in his dealings with Parliament. The most senior ministers recognized that she was really in charge.

Like father, like son

Although he hated his father, George became more and more like him as he got older. His court became as boring as George I's had been, and he came to develop the same preference for his Hanoverian lands that his father had felt. He declared he was, "sick to death" of British ways, and wanted to stay in Hanover permanently.

Fights and feuds

George was bad-tempered too, continuing the tradition of family feuding. He couldn't stand his eldest son, Frederick, and the two rowed furiously. Caroline also loathed her first-born, calling him the, "greatest beast in the whole world". George wouldn't even let Frederick see his mother as she was dying – much to Caroline's relief.

Bonnie Prince Charlie

Decades after the failure of the 1715 uprising led by James Stuart, the Jacobites fixed their hopes on James's son, Charles, nicknamed 'Bonnie Prince Charlie'.

Led by Charles, the Jacobites invaded England in 1745. But they were soon on the run from government troops. The two sides fought the battle of Culloden in Scotland in April 1746.

The Jacobites lost the battle, and Charles went into hiding. He eventually escaped from Scotland dressed as a maid, and fled to France.

GEORGE III
1760-1820

Born: June 4, 1738

Married: Charlotte of Meklenburg-Strelitz, September 8, 1761

Crowned: September 22, 1761

Died: January 29, 1820

George III was a popular king whose reign was marred by the loss of Britain's American colonies and by his illness.

Rustic royalty

The King became known as 'Farmer George' because of his interest in the latest trends in farming.

He would wander around his estates, chatting to anyone he saw working there.

FARMER GEORGE

George II's son, Frederick, died of pneumonia nine years before his father. So when the King had a fatal heart attack in 1760, it was Frederick's eldest son, yet another George, who succeeded him.

But George III was nothing like the previous two Georges. He was only 22 when he became King. He had been born in London, and was proud to be British, refusing even to visit his Hanoverian lands.

An idealistic ruler

Although he was young, George had a keen sense of his kingly responsibilities. Deeply religious and hard-working, he believed that Parliament had become much too powerful under his predecessors. As soon as he became King, he started trying to reclaim power for the throne, by forcing ministers to accept his trusted adviser, the Earl of Bute, as Prime Minister.

Art, music and science

George also saw it as his duty to support the arts. An enthusiastic artist, he helped found the Royal Academy of Arts in 1768. And, although he hadn't been studious as a boy, he became fascinated by science, botany and astronomy, supporting experts in these fields, too.

The King built up a huge library. Eventually, he amassed over 65,000 volumes – one of the largest collections ever gathered by one person. These were made freely available for scholars to read, and today they fill six floors of a tower in the British Library.

A family man

The new King married just two weeks before his coronation. He met his bride, a young German princess named Charlotte, only hours before their wedding, but the couple fell in love. They tried to live a normal life together, calling each other Mr. and Mrs. King in private.

As well as being a caring husband, George was a loving, if often overbearing, father to their 15 children.

Dull and respectable

The upper classes soon became bored with the new King, whose rather homely interests they didn't share. But on the whole, the British public quickly came to like George, seeing him as down-to-earth and honest.

Fit for a king

Big, fancy meals were all the rage among the British nobility – but the King and his wife preferred plain, healthy food, and not too much of it. His eating habits were often mocked for being cheap and frugal.

This picture shows George and his family, dressed in costumes based on those worn during Charles I's reign. The future George IV is on the left in red, and William IV is holding a bird.

This picture shows New York rebels toppling a gilded statue of George III in 1776. The metal statue was melted down and turned into weapons.

Deadly poison

A lock of George's hair was recently found to hold high levels of a poison called arsenic. At the time, this was used in wig powder, skin cream and some medicines.

Arsenic may have contributed to many illnesses among the rich, before people realized how dangerous it could be.

Revolution in America

Britain ruled colonies in many continents. But, by the 1770s, people in the 13 North American colonies were becoming angry that they had to pay very high taxes to Britain yet had no representatives in Parliament in London. This anger soon turned to revolt.

Fighting went on for years, but in 1783 the British government finally recognized American independence. George III was so devastated at losing America that, for a while, he considered stepping down as King.

The King's madness

In 1788, the King developed an alarming illness. He frothed at the mouth, spoke nonsense and became confused. This 'madness' passed quickly, but he suffered from further attacks in 1801 and 1804. Many experts now think his symptoms were caused by a condition known as porphyria.

Republicanism

In 1789, a revolution broke out in France, which ended with the execution of the French King and Queen and the abolition of the monarchy.

This inspired a group of rebels in Ireland. At that time, Ireland was still ruled by Britain. The Irish had their own Parliament, but the country's Catholic majority only had very limited rights. The rebels wanted to break away and set up an independent republic, ruled by elected leaders rather than a monarch, where Catholics would be treated more fairly.

They launched an uprising in 1798. The French sent troops to help, but they didn't arrive in time, and the rebellion was soon crushed.

United Kingdom

To prevent further uprisings, the British government introduced the Act of Union in 1801. It joined Ireland and Britain into a new United Kingdom, under one parliament, promising better rights for Catholics. But, in the end, the King, who was a staunch Protestant, refused to pass the law giving Catholics extra rights.

Regency years

In 1810, George suffered another bout of madness. From 1811, it was clear that he was no longer fit to run the kingdom. Instead, his eldest son, George, the Prince of Wales, took over as regent.

The King never recovered. Eventually, he became blind and delirious, and could no longer recognize his family. He finally died of pneumonia in January 1820.

The Union flag

A flag was designed for the newly-formed United Kingdom. It merged the British and Irish flags to create the flag that is used today.

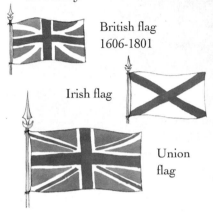

British flag 1606-1801

Irish flag

Union flag

Napoleonic wars

From 1796, a brilliant French commander named Napoleon Bonaparte fought to establish French control over Europe.

The British and their allies defeated him at the Battle of Trafalgar in 1805, and beat him for good at Waterloo in 1815. This helped to restore George's popularity after the loss of America.

In this cartoon, George is shown as a gentle giant, observing a savage Napoleon.

GEORGE IV
1820-1830

Born: August 12, 1762

Married: Caroline of
Brunswick, April 8, 1795

Regent from: 1811

Crowned: July 19, 1821

Died: June 26, 1830

George IV was a decadent and
unpopular king, but his reign
was an era of great culture.

This flattering portrait of
George IV was painted in
1822, by which time the
King was actually very
overweight.

THE BIG SPENDER

George III's eldest son, George, ruled the country as
Prince Regent for 10 years before he became King.
Known as 'Prinny', he was clever, but he was also
greedy, lazy and extravagant. The public came to hate
him for his spendthrift ways.

An unfortunate union

As a young man, George had a string of scandalous
affairs. In 1785, he even secretly married a Catholic
woman named Maria Fitzherbert, although the
marriage was illegal as the King hadn't approved it.

In 1795, Prince George allowed his father to choose
a wife for him, in return for Parliament's help in paying
off his growing debts. The King chose Princess
Caroline of Brunswick, in order to forge a political
union with her German homeland.

But George and Caroline detested each other
from first sight. She was loud, tactless and
didn't wash; he was far less attractive than
she'd been expecting. After their
wedding, the two avoided spending
any time together.

Powerful Parliament

As soon as George became Prince
Regent, he tried to divorce Caroline,
but Parliament wouldn't allow it.
George was furious, but all he could
do was rant and rage. True power by
now lay with Parliament.

Making a scene

In 1820, George became King. He staged a spectacular coronation at Westminster Abbey, with lavish costumes costing tens of thousands of pounds.

At one point, Caroline arrived at the Abbey, to stake her claim as Queen. She pounded on the doors demanding to be let in, but George had ordered guards to keep her out. Deeply humiliated, she left, and died a few weeks later.

A man of taste

George was wildly extravagant, but he also bought many fine paintings that are now part of the Royal Collection. And he supported the finest architects of his day, allowing them to develop an elegant style of townhouse that still survives across much of Britain.

Lonely last days

As George grew older, he became reclusive. Bloated and ill from decades of overindulgence, he died in 1830. He wasn't mourned – one newspaper wrote: "There never was an individual less regretted by his fellow creatures than this
    deceased king."

Brighton

As Prince Regent, George spent lots of time in the seaside town of Brighton. Soon, all high society flocked there too.

George owned a farmhouse in Brighton, but it was too simple for his tastes. So he rebuilt it in an extraordinary mix of oriental styles, creating a fitting venue for his glamorous parties.

But the new building, Brighton Pavilion, wasn't finished until 1823. By then, George was tiring of his old ways. He only visited the completed Pavilion twice.

Today, Brighton Pavilion is a popular tourist attraction, owned by the town of Brighton.

WILLIAM IV
1830-1837

Born: August 21, 1765

Married: Adelaide of
Saxe-Meiningen,
July 11, 1818

Crowned: September 8,
1831

Died: June 20, 1837

An ex-sailor, William was 64
when he became King. He was
mocked for being old and
out of touch.

THE SAILOR KING

Geoorge IV and Caroline only had one child – Princess
Charlotte, who had died in 1817. So when George
died, his 64-year-old brother William became King.

Career and family

As the third son of George III, for most of his life
William hadn't expected to become King. He had
joined the navy aged 13 and, after a long career, he had
settled down with an actress known as Mrs. Jordan.
They had ten children but never married, which meant
their children couldn't succeed to the throne.

Soon after Princess Charlotte died, William married
a young German princess named Adelaide. He hoped
they would have children, who would be able to inherit
the throne. But their two daughters died as infants, and
the couple remained childless. Still, Adelaide was a
kind stepmother to William's many children.

This unflattering cartoon
shows William, Mrs. Jordan
and some of their children.

Before he became King,
William was the Duke of
Clarence, and his children
were known as
the 'Fitzclarences'.

Different brothers

William was totally unlike his extravagant brother. Bluff and straightforward, he didn't care for ceremony. He would talk to anyone he met in the street, swore like the sailor he was, and often spat in public.

He also had no time for money-wasters, and insisted that his coronation in 1831 should cost just a tenth of what his brother's had done.

Out of touch

At first, William's simple tastes went down well with his subjects. But they soon became frustrated by him. Old and stubborn, he was often out of touch with the times. He was reluctant to support popular measures, such as the ending of the slave trade, and was slow to encourage reforms that would make elections fairer and give more people the vote.

These changes went through, despite William's complaints. It was becoming clear that the monarchy had less and less influence over political decisions.

This portrait shows William in his naval uniform. He was a friend of Admiral Nelson, who defeated Napoleon at the Battle of Trafalgar in 1805.

End of the line

William's heir was his young niece, Victoria. He was fond of her, but couldn't stand her mother, who he considered arrogant and rude.

William knew that if he died before Victoria turned 18, then her mother would rule as regent. He was determined not to let that happen. So, even though he became very ill, he clung onto life until June 1837 – just a month after Victoria's 18th birthday.

Key events

• September 1830 – one of the first railway lines was opened, between Liverpool and Manchester.

• June 1832 – the Reform Act gave the vote to an extra 500,000 people.

• August 1834 – slavery was abolished in most of the British Empire.

• October 1834 – the Houses of Parliament burned down.

This portrait of the young Princess was made when she was around nine years old. Although she looks like a little lady in the picture, at the time her mother was struggling for money.

ENGLAND'S ROSE

Victoria was hardly more than a girl when she became Queen, and her youth and femininity helped to endear her to the British public. The new Queen's reign was to span over 60 years. During that period, Britain became a major industrial power, and came to control a huge empire.

Lonely girl

Victoria was born in 1819, and christened Alexandrina Victoria. Her father, George III's fourth son, died when she was just eight months old, leaving her and her mother without much money. They had to live in a decaying set of old royal apartments in Kensington Palace. To make matters worse, her mother was very protective, and kept her away from other children.

Despite her lonely childhood, the young Victoria grew up lively and headstrong. She was determined to serve her country well when she became Queen.

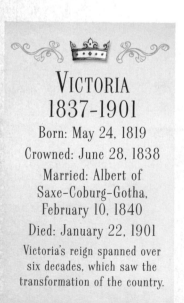

VICTORIA
1837-1901

Born: May 24, 1819

Crowned: June 28, 1838

Married: Albert of Saxe-Coburg-Gotha, February 10, 1840

Died: January 22, 1901

Victoria's reign spanned over six decades, which saw the transformation of the country.

Queen Victoria

One summer's night in 1837, the 18-year-old heir was woken to be told her that her uncle, William IV, had died. Although dishevelled and dressed in her nightclothes, she received the news gracefully. When she first signed her name as Queen, she used only her middle name, and was ever after known as Queen Victoria.

Her first act as Queen was to free herself from her mother's clutches. She moved to Buckingham Palace, and relied on the Prime Minister, rather than her mother, to advise her – to her mother's disappointment.

Early years

The build-up to the Queen's coronation was celebrated with exhibitions, concerts, and balls, at which Victoria was the star guest. The coronation itself was a grand occasion, and Victoria's small, dignified figure – she was only 5ft (1.5m tall) – impressed the crowds.

Choosing a husband

Victoria met her quiet, handsome German cousin, Albert of Saxe-Coburg-Gotha, when she was 17. She fell in love with him, describing him as, "perfection in every way". In 1839 she asked him to marry her – as Queen, she had to ask – and he agreed. They were married the following year, on a rainy February day.

Albert proved to be a loving husband and father. Although he didn't hold much power, he was a constant support to his wife, and acted as her secretary.

White wedding

Victoria was married in a white wedding dress, made of satin and decorated with orange blossoms and lace.

It set the custom for white wedding dresses – before that, brides usually just wore their best dress.

This portrait of Victoria, Albert and some of their children was painted in 1846. Their eldest son, the future Edward VII, stands by Victoria's knee.

Giant greenhouse

Crystal Palace, shown in the picture above, was built specially for the Great Exhibition.

Victoria described the opening of the exhibition as, "the proudest day of my life". She visited 13 times with her family.

Exhibits included farm tools, sewing looms, and steam engines.

The Great Exhibition

Still, Albert wanted to prove himself to be more than just Victoria's husband. He started planning a massive exhibition to celebrate technology and industry. The collection of over 13,000 items from around the world was to be housed in a gigantic glass building, known as the Crystal Palace, in Hyde Park in London.

This 'Great Exhibition' opened in May 1851. By the time it closed in October, over 6 million people had visited, and similar projects were being planned in New York and Munich. After Albert's success, he was given the new title of 'Prince Consort', in recognition of his importance to the country and to the Queen.

New museums

The Great Exhibition made a huge profit which was used to found a museum complex in nearby South Kensington. This was made up of what became the Natural History Museum, the Science Museum and the Victoria and Albert Museum.

Growing family

Victoria and Albert had nine children, although Victoria hated pregnancy – she said that it made her feel, "like a cow or a dog". During the birth of her later children, she took chloroform to relieve the pain. Her example helped to make the use of painkillers in childbirth increasingly commonplace.

The royal couple tried to spend as much time living as a normal family as possible, at their private country homes, Osborne House on the Isle of Wight and Balmoral Castle in Scotland. They came to represent the ideal Victorian family in the eyes of the public.

A widow queen

But their happy life came to an end suddenly in 1861, when the 42-year-old Albert died of typhoid fever. Victoria was beyond heartbroken. For the next decade, she shut herself away, struggling to cope with her grief. Ministers mostly had to communicate with her in writing and for several years she wouldn't even open Parliament – her most important royal duty.

Sympathy for her soon ran dry. Many journalists and politicians questioned whether Britain even needed a monarch at all.

A Christmas king

Many modern Christmas traditions in Britain were introduced from Germany by Prince Albert, including...

... decorating a Christmas tree...

... and sending Christmas cards.

Victoria is shown here in black mourning clothes, with her servant John Brown. They became very close after Albert's death.

Changing world

Victoria's reign was a time of great progress when all sorts of new inventions changed the way people lived:

- steam engines
- telegraphs
- electric lights
- gramophones
- telephones
- typewriters
- photography
- bicycles

Back to work

By the late 1860s, Victoria had recovered enough to start appearing in public again. But she never got over Albert's death. She wore mourning black for the rest of her life, and named a series of monuments after him, including the Albert Memorial and Royal Albert Hall.

Head of an empire

During Victoria's reign, the British extended their overseas Empire until it was so vast that it was said the sun never set on it – it was always daytime somewhere. Victoria became the figurehead of this powerful Empire, and took the title 'Empress of India' in 1877.

The pink areas on this Victorian world map show the extent of the British Empire in 1886.

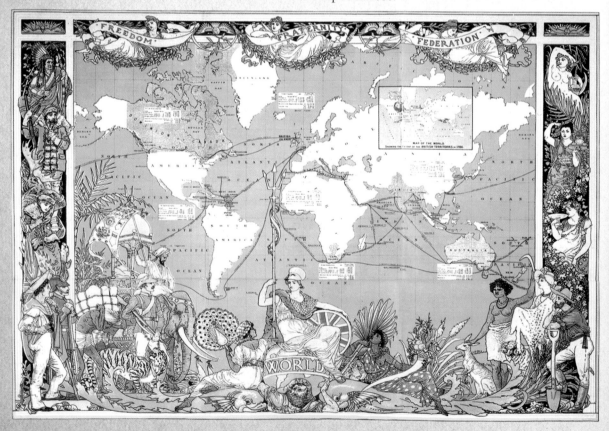

Jubilee celebrations

In June 1887, Victoria's 50th year as
Queen was marked with huge Golden
Jubilee celebrations, including a grand
banquet and an enormous procession
through the streets London.

Over half a million people flocked
to the capital, to stand in the sun, listen
to the bands, and applaud and wave
flags as the Queen's gilded carriage
went past.

Her Diamond Jubilee ten years
later was even more spectacular. Huge
crowds lined the streets of London to
catch a glimpse of Victoria as she passed.
The Queen, by this time old and frail,
was so moved by their deafening cheers
and singing that she wept.

End of an age

In 1901, Victoria died, aged 81. It was the end of an
era during which Britain had become the world's
leading industrial nation and had come to rule over the
largest empire ever seen.

At her request, the Queen, who had worn
mourning black for nearly half her life, was buried in a
white dress. With her in her coffin were her wedding
veil and Albert's old dressing gown. On February 4,
1901, she was finally laid to rest next to her beloved
Albert. The two still lie in the mausoleum she had built
for them in the quiet, peaceful gardens of Frogmore
House, near Windsor Castle.

Grandmother of Europe

This photograph shows
Victoria in 1894 with her
son, grandson and great-
grandson, the future Kings
Edward VII, George V and
Edward VIII.

Most of Victoria's children
married members of
European royal families.

She had over 30
grandchildren, and became
known as the 'Grandmama
of Europe'.

THE PEACEMAKER

Edward VII was 59 years old when he became King. His mother, Queen Victoria, had ruled successfully for 64 years, and he knew it would be no easy task to follow in her steps.

Disappointing son

Edward was christened Albert Edward, and was known to family and friends as 'Bertie'. Victoria had hoped that he would take after her serious, moral husband. But much to her disapproval, he loved parties, fashion and feasting.

When he was 20, the prince had an affair with an actress. The scandal deeply shocked his father and may have hastened his death. Victoria never forgave her son. In 1863, Bertie married the kind, beautiful Alexandra of Denmark. He had mistresses for the rest of his life, but she always claimed he loved her the best.

This impressive portrait shows Edward in his grand coronation robes.

Edward understood the power of appearances, and he took great care to present and dress himself well.

EDWARD VII
1901-1910

Born: November 9, 1841

Married: Alexandra of Denmark, March 10, 1863

Crowned: August 9, 1902

Died: May 6, 1910

Edward was a very charming king who strengthened Britain's foreign relations.

A new style

When he became King, Bertie had little experience, as Victoria had refused to give him many duties. But he proved far more capable than Victoria could ever have thought possible. He quickly distanced himself from his mother's austere reign, and discarded his father's name Albert to take the title 'Edward VII'.

Edward also staged a grand, theatrical coronation, and set about redecorating the old-fashioned royal residences to make them stylish and elegant. His new, energetic ways soon made him popular with the public.

Friends abroad

Edward's diplomatic skills were first put to the test during Victoria's reign, when he visited India, Canada, and the United States. Everywhere he went, his easy, courteous manner, honed from decades of hosting parties, strengthened Britain's foreign relations.

During his own reign, Edward continued to win friends and allies. In 1903, he visited France. Relations between France and Britain were poor at that time. But he was so charming that by the end of his stay, he was cheered in the streets. He also persuaded the French president to sign an agreement, the *Entente Cordiale*, French for 'friendly understanding'. This guaranteed that Britain and France would support each other in future conflicts.

Death and mourning

Edward ate huge meals every day, and smoked dozens of cigars. He paid the price for his unhealthy ways in 1910, when he died after suffering several heart attacks.

Thousands of mourners, including leaders from across Europe, turned out to watch the King's funeral procession as it made its way from London to Windsor.

Sandringham

In 1862, Victoria bought a house at Sandringham, in Norfolk, for her son.

Edward and his wife arranged for it to be rebuilt as a luxurious, airy mansion, complete with a bowling alley and a farm on the grounds.

The clocks at Sandringham were set half an hour fast, so winter afternoons would seem to stay lighter for longer. This allowed Edward and his friends more time to stay out shooting.

Sandringham is still owned by the royal family today, who stay there each New Year.

When they're not there, it's open to the public.

A modern dynasty

In 1917, Queen Victoria's grandson, George V, changed the royal family's name from Saxe-Coburg-Gotha to Windsor. The family has used that name ever since.

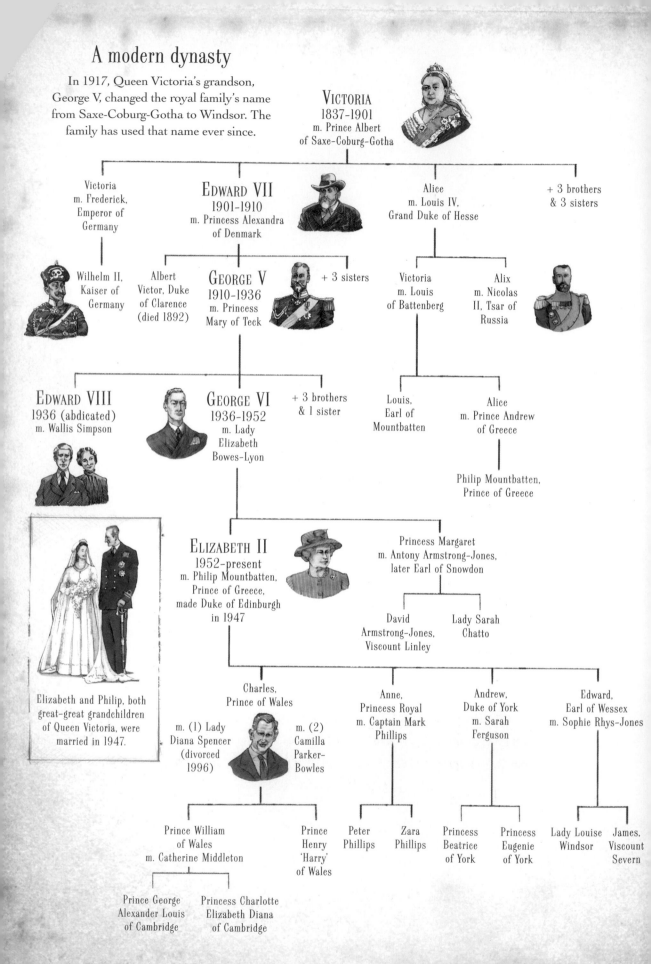

VICTORIA
1837-1901
m. Prince Albert of Saxe-Coburg-Gotha

Victoria
m. Frederick, Emperor of Germany

EDWARD VII
1901-1910
m. Princess Alexandra of Denmark

Alice
m. Louis IV, Grand Duke of Hesse

+ 3 brothers & 3 sisters

Wilhelm II, Kaiser of Germany

Albert Victor, Duke of Clarence (died 1892)

GEORGE V
1910-1936
m. Princess Mary of Teck

+ 3 sisters

Victoria
m. Louis of Battenberg

Alix
m. Nicolas II, Tsar of Russia

EDWARD VIII
1936 (abdicated)
m. Wallis Simpson

GEORGE VI
1936-1952
m. Lady Elizabeth Bowes-Lyon

+ 3 brothers & 1 sister

Louis, Earl of Mountbatten

Alice
m. Prince Andrew of Greece

Philip Mountbatten, Prince of Greece

ELIZABETH II
1952-present
m. Philip Mountbatten, Prince of Greece, made Duke of Edinburgh in 1947

Princess Margaret
m. Antony Armstrong-Jones, later Earl of Snowdon

David Armstrong-Jones, Viscount Linley

Lady Sarah Chatto

Elizabeth and Philip, both great-great grandchildren of Queen Victoria, were married in 1947.

Charles, Prince of Wales

m. (1) Lady Diana Spencer (divorced 1996)

m. (2) Camilla Parker-Bowles

Anne, Princess Royal
m. Captain Mark Phillips

Andrew, Duke of York
m. Sarah Ferguson

Edward, Earl of Wessex
m. Sophie Rhys-Jones

Prince William of Wales
m. Catherine Middleton

Prince Henry 'Harry' of Wales

Peter Phillips

Zara Phillips

Princess Beatrice of York

Princess Eugenie of York

Lady Louise Windsor

James, Viscount Severn

Prince George Alexander Louis of Cambridge

Princess Charlotte Elizabeth Diana of Cambridge

THE WINDSORS

With the rapid growth of the media since the early 20th century, it's easier than ever for modern monarchs to reach the public. But it's much harder for them to control the way they are portrayed or to protect their privacy.

The Windsors have faced many personal challenges under the public eye. They've made a few mistakes along the way, but they have modernized the monarchy and brought it into the 21st century.

GEORGE V
1910–1936

Born: June 3, 1865

Married: Princess Mary of Teck, July 6, 1893

Crowned: Westminster Abbey, June 22, 1911

Died: January 20, 1936

Changed the royal family's name to Windsor during the First World War.

In 1932, he became the first British monarch to make a Christmas broadcast on the radio.

An enthusiastic sailor, George V is shown at the wheel of his yacht in this photograph.

George served 14 years in the Royal Navy. He loved the discipline of naval life, and it took him to all corners of the British Empire.

REBRANDING THE ROYALS

After Edward VII died, the new King, George V, wrote in his diary, "I have lost my best friend and the best of fathers." They had been close, but George was very different. Bluff and practical, with a tendency to swear, he preferred staying in with his stamp collection to being the focus at official occasions.

Despite his conservative nature, George went on to modernize the royal family during a time of rapid social change that brought many other monarchies to an end.

International relations

George was closely related to most of the royal families of Europe. As a child, he spent summers in Denmark, his mother's homeland. There, he went fishing with his cousins, the future German ruler, Kaiser Wilhelm, and the future Tsar Nicholas of Russia.

When he was 12, George and his elder brother, Albert, joined the navy. In 1892, he was at sea when he heard that Albert had died, and he was now his father's heir.

The tide turns

By the time George became King, in 1910, political relations between Britain and Germany had become strained. But he believed his family ties, and Britain's naval power, were strong enough to prevent a war. The outbreak of the First World War in 1914 proved him wrong. With Germany up against Britain, Russia and France, the cousins were at war.

George and his wife, Queen Mary, immediately threw themselves into the war effort, making hundreds of visits to meet workers in munitions factories and wounded servicemen in hospitals. The King himself made over 450 visits to troops on the front line.

Despite all this, George was criticized because of his German connection. So, in July 1917, he changed his family name from 'Saxe-Coburg-Gotha' to 'Windsor'.

Time for change

The War led to lots of changes. Many now questioned the old order – and whether there was any point in kings and queens. People in Ireland and the colonies of the British Empire called for independence, and workers demanded more rights. The King, who had once captained ships, steered the monarchy through these upheavals, often acting as a mediator in disputes.

In May 1935, street parties were held across the land to celebrate George V's Silver Jubilee. Just six months later, this popular but unassuming King died.

During his last years, George had become increasingly worried about his flighty son, Edward. "After I am dead," the King said, "the boy will ruin himself in 12 months." Sadly, he was proved right.

Events of George V's reign

1912 Passenger liner, *Titanic*, sinks on its first voyage.

1912 Captain Scott's expedition reaches the South Pole, but none of the group survives.

1914-1918 The First World War

1917 Gandhi begins campaigning for India's independence.

1918 Russian revolutionaries execute Tsar Nicolas and his family.

1921 Southern Ireland becomes independent.

1922 The BBC is founded.

1926 British workers hold a General Strike.

1928 British women over 21 gain the vote.

1929 Wall Street Crash in New York leads to global economic depression.

1931 The Statute of Westminster gives British colonies greater independence.

EDWARD VIII
January–December
1936

Born: Richmond, Surrey
June 23, 1884

Abdicated: Dec 10, 1936

Died: Paris, May 28, 1972

Stepped down from
the throne to marry
Wallis Simpson.

Personality clash

As a young man, Edward didn't get along with his father, George V. He deliberately indulged in activities that he knew would annoy the King:

learning
to fly...

steeplechase
racing...

and taking lots
of holidays.

KING FOR A YEAR

"I have found it impossible to carry the heavy burden of responsibility and to discharge my duties as King as I would wish to do without the help and support of the woman I love." On December 11, 1936, a stunned nation tuned into their radios to hear these words, as Edward VIII announced that he had quit the throne.

Youthful folly

The eldest son of George V, Edward, was known to his family as David, which was actually his last name. Intelligent but easily bored, his school results were poor. In 1912, he went to Oxford University, where he excelled at partying and hunting, but not at studying.

Two years later, the First World War broke out. Like many young men, Edward joined the army, eager to fight for his country. But, much to his annoyance, he was kept safely behind the front line.

Courting trouble

After the War, Edward went on official tours around the world, where his dashing good looks and roguish charm proved popular. Meanwhile, he had a string of scandalous affairs with older, married women. Then in 1931, he met Wallis Simpson, an American living in London with her second husband. A romance blossomed, and it soon became serious.

On January 20, 1936, Edward came to the throne. Around this time, Mrs. Simpson divorced her husband. Now Edward was determined to make her his wife and his Queen.

Fall from grace

But not even kings can always have it their own way. The Prime Minister told Edward that Parliament wouldn't accept Mrs. Simpson as Queen, so he'd have to choose between her and the crown – he chose her. The day after announcing his decision to the people, he left the country. Apart from two brief visits home, he would spend the rest of his life in exile.

Tea with Hitler

Edward – now the Duke of Windsor – married Mrs. Simpson in France in June 1937. Later that year, they visited Germany, where they went to tea with the country's leader, Adolf Hitler. War with Germany was already brewing, so this caused outrage in Britain. Two years later, the Second World War broke out. Amid concerns about Edward's apparent support for Hitler, and a German plot to kidnap him and make him King again, the British government made him governor of the Bahamas and packed him off to the Caribbean out of harm's way.

After the War, Edward retired to Paris, where he spent the rest of his days. The exiled King died from throat cancer in 1972, when he finally returned home to be buried in the royal burial ground at Frogmore.

Edward and Wallis pose, unsmiling, for their wedding photograph. The royal family refused to attend and made it clear that Wallis would have no royal status.

Why abdicate?

If Edward had married Wallis without giving up the throne he'd have been in an impossible position.

As King, he was head of the Church of England, which was opposed to divorce. What's more, if he'd gone against his ministers' advice, the government would have had to resign, sparking a major political crisis.

GEORGE VI
1936-52

Born: December 14, 1895

Married: Lady Elizabeth
Bowes-Lyon, April 26, 1923

Crowned: Westminster
Abbey, May 12, 1937

Died: February 6, 1952

Served in the navy and
air force during the
First World War.

Played doubles in the tennis
championships at Wimbledon
in 1926.

KING IN WARTIME

The royal family's reputation was in pieces after the abdication. Edward's brother became George VI, and it was up to him to restore public faith in the monarchy. But it would be a hard task. Having grown up in Edward's shadow, he'd had no training for kingship. He was quiet and shy, with a stammer that made public speaking a torment for him.

Crowned on the day originally set for Edward's coronation, one of the first things George did as King was to cut all contact with his brother, refusing to take his telephone calls. Relations remained frosty between them after that, but it was a sensible move. To those who felt let down by Edward's abdication it was a clear sign that King George meant business.

Keeping up morale during the Blitz, the King and Queen share a joke with the locals in London's East End.

Like father, like son

The new King – known as 'Bertie' to his family – had been christened Albert Frederick Arthur George. But, now, he took his father's name as a sign of continuity. Dull, but dependable, he had more in common with his father than with his brother.

Blitz spirit

Like George V before him, George VI's reign was overshadowed by the outbreak of another world war. Believing that the Prime Minister, Winston Churchill, would lead the country to victory, George worked tirelessly to keep up public morale.

Many of Britain's cities suffered heavy bombing during the Second World War. Buckingham Palace itself was hit nine times, but the royal family steadfastly refused to leave London. The King and Queen won the hearts of the nation, visiting people in the areas worst hit by the bombs. George even battled against his stammer and his fear of public speaking, to make radio broadcasts giving hope and encouragement to the people at home and the troops on the front line.

End game

After the War, many of Britain's remaining colonies became independent. Most stayed part of the Commonwealth, with the King at its head, working to promote peace and co-operation between its members. George VI had brought the monarchy new strength and purpose, but the stresses of kingship had taken their toll. On February 6, 1952, he died at the age of 56.

"Us four"

Kingship didn't come naturally to George VI. Luckily, he had the love and support of a strong wife who helped him grow more confident in public, and a close-knit family that gave him a happy home life.

The couple had two daughters, Elizabeth – known as 'Lilibet' – and Margaret Rose. George referred to the family as "us four" and tried to give the princesses as normal a life as possible.

He gave them their first corgi dogs as pets in 1933. Elizabeth has had corgis ever since.

ELIZABETH II
1952-present

Born: April 21, 1926

Married: Philip Mountbatten, November 20, 1947

Ascended to throne: February 6, 1952

Crowned: Westminster Abbey, June 2, 1953

In the course of her long reign, Elizabeth II has met more heads of state than any previous monarch.

"I declare before you all that my whole life, whether it be long or short, shall be devoted to your service."

Part of Elizabeth's 21st birthday speech, broadcast in 1947

Elizabeth was at Treetops Hotel, in Kenya, when she heard the news that her father had died.

DEVOTED TO SERVICE

From an early age, George VI's elder daughter, Elizabeth, took her royal duties very seriously.

To prepare her for her future role, she was given lessons in constitutional history and law, alongside the usual school subjects. Elizabeth also took on many royal duties while she was still a teenager, making her first radio broadcast when she was just 14 years old.

Hard-working and conscientious, her childhood motto, "I must not take the easy way out," is one that she's stuck to throughout her life.

Sharing the burden

Elizabeth was 13 when the Second World War broke out. She and her younger sister, Margaret, moved from Buckingham Palace to the relative safety of Windsor Castle.

They may have been princesses, but they were still expected to make do on limited rations of food, fuel and clothing, like everyone else. The King even marked a line on their baths, to make sure they were never filled any deeper than 13cm (5 inches). When she was 19, Elizabeth joined the Auxiliary Services as a mechanic.

Celebrating peace

On May 8, 1945, she stood with the King and Winston Churchill on the balcony of Buckingham Palace to greet the crowds celebrating the end of the War in Europe. Later, she and Princess Margaret mingled anonymously with the merrymakers below.

A family affair

In July 1947, Elizabeth announced her engagement to Prince Philip of Greece and Denmark. The couple had met shortly before the War and it was love at first sight.

They were married that November at Westminster Abbey. Clothing was still rationed at the time, so even Elizabeth had to save clothing coupons for her wedding dress.

A year later, the couple had their first child, Charles, followed by Anne in 1950, Andrew in 1960 and Edward in 1964.

A crowning moment

After George VI's death, Elizabeth flew home from a tour, to embark on her new role. Her coronation, on June 2, 1953, was a sumptuous affair, watched on television by over twenty million Britons. Many bought their first ever TV sets specially for the occasion.

To a nation that was still recovering from the war, the coronation was cause for celebration and hope for a brighter future.

This coronation portrait of Elizabeth was taken by Cecil Beaton. The Queen is pictured wearing the Imperial State Crown, and holding the Sceptre and the Orb (see page 173).

Commonwealth

The Queen has visited every country in the Commonwealth (except for Cameroon, which joined in 1995). She also attends its Heads of Government meetings.

The Commonwealth unites a third of the world's population living in countries that used to be part of the British Empire.

ROYAL PAGEANTS

Since the early days of her reign, Queen Elizabeth has been in the public eye. She has opened public buildings, watched parades and attended national and international ceremonies.

Her engagements as monarch have been reported daily in the Court Circular section of newspapers, and relayed to the world via television sets and, more recently, her very own website.

On tour

By royal car, train, helicopter, plane and yacht, Elizabeth has visited more places around the world and met more heads of state than any other monarch. On trips at home and abroad, she has greeted the crowds face-to-face as part of the 'Royal walkabout' – a custom that she personally introduced.

The royal family gathers on the balcony of Buckingham Palace after Charles and Diana's wedding.

Silver celebrations

The 25th year of Queen Elizabeth's reign was marked by Silver Jubilee celebrations in 1977. Across Britain, a chain of bonfires was lit, and parties were held in neighbourhood streets.

However, tragedy followed close behind, when a bomb, planted by Irish terrorists, killed Prince Philip's uncle, Lord Mountbatten, in 1979.

Wedding bells

The country was united in celebration once again for the marriage of Elizabeth's eldest son, Prince Charles, to Lady Diana Spencer, on July 29, 1981. Over 750 million people around the world watched the fairy-tale ceremony, broadcast live from St. Paul's Cathedral. The births of Princes William and Harry followed soon after, in 1982 and 1984.

On parade

Although Elizabeth's birthday is in April, it's officially marked in June, with a parade known as Trooping the Colour.

Troops from the army's Household Division line up for a royal inspection.

Military bands play while the 'colours' (flags) are 'trooped' (carried) down the ranks.

The Queen then rides to Buckingham Palace to watch a Royal Air Force fly-past from the balcony.

Safe as houses?

The Windsors have been more accessible to the public than previous monarchs, but some people have come too close for comfort.

In 1974, a gunman stopped Princess Anne's car. Ian Ball attempted to kidnap her, and demanded £2million. He shot and wounded two police officers, Anne's driver and a journalist before he was arrested.

Queen Elizabeth woke one morning, in 1982, to find a stranger in her room. The intruder, Michael Fagan, sat on the bed and talked to her for 10 minutes before security guards arrived.

In 2003, comedian Aaron Barschak gatecrashed Prince William's 21st birthday party, disguised as Osama bin Laden in a party dress.

GOOD TIMES AND BAD

Queen Elizabeth has weathered many storms as head of 'the Firm' – the royal family's own name for itself. The private lives of her children were the cause of particular troubles in the 1980s and '90s. Journalists criticized their relationships and lifestyles, and accused them of neglecting their royal duties, as the public mood towards the royal family began to sour.

"A horrible year"

"It has turned out to be an *annus horribilis*," remarked Elizabeth at the end of 1992. She had been on the throne for 40 years, but there was little to celebrate.

In the course of the year, the marriages of her children, Anne, Andrew and Charles, all ended. Then, on November 20, a fire at Windsor Castle swept through over 100 historic rooms. Fortunately, no one was killed or seriously injured, but the repairs took five years and cost £37million to complete.

Another turn for the worse

On August 31, 1997, Prince Charles's former wife, Diana, was killed in a car crash in Paris. Her death shocked and obsessed the world.

Before the funeral, the Queen stayed with her grandsons, William and Harry, in Balmoral, away from the attention of the public. It was an unpopular decision. Demands were made, even by the Prime Minister, that she mourn in the capital instead. Elizabeth listened, moved the family to London and broadcast an address to the nation.

Golden Age

In 2002, Queen Elizabeth celebrated her Golden Jubilee – 50 years as Queen. But the year began sadly. Elizabeth's sister, Princess Margaret, and the Queen Mother both died within weeks of each other.

The jubilee festivities went ahead all the same. There were parades across the Commonwealth, and two special nights of music were held in the gardens of Buckingham Palace. A recording of the pop concert sold so well that the Queen became the first monarch or member of the royal family to receive a gold disc. The public's affection had been reaffirmed, and Elizabeth spoke of the "gratitude, respect and pride" that she felt for her subjects.

Long to reign

After all the ups and downs of her reign, Queen Elizabeth remains one of the country's longest serving monarchs, and one of the most respected.

The Queen Mum

Born:
August 4, 1900

Died:
March 30, 2002

Adolf Hitler described her as "the most dangerous woman in Europe", while Wallis Simpson nicknamed her "Cookie".

In later years, her sense of fun and her love of horse racing endeared her to the public as the nation's granny.

After her death, over 200,000 people visited Westminster Hall, where her body lay in state for 3 days.

Happy crowds gather outside Buckingham Palace, which is lit up for the Queen's Golden Jubilee celebrations.

Princes of Wales

In 1301, Edward I made his son, Edward, Prince of Wales. He was the first English heir to the throne to be given the title.

Charles was crowned Prince of Wales on July 1, 1969 at an investiture ceremony at Caernarfon Castle. There he addressed the crowds in both English and Welsh, which he had learned especially for the occasion.

WORKING FOR THE FIRM

On September 9, 2015, Queen Elizabeth surpassed her great-grandmother Queen Victoria's record, to become Britain's longest-reigning monarch. While she continues to carry out her royal duties, she is now supported by other members of the royal family, who attend many public engagements on her behalf.

Next in line

A crucial royal duty has always been to secure the future of the royal family by producing heirs. As the Queen's eldest son, Prince Charles is first in line to the throne. His elder son, Prince William, is second in line. In April 2011, William married Catherine Middleton. They are now known as the Duke and Duchess of Cambridge, and had their first child, George, in 2013 followed by Charlotte in 2015.

Prince William and his wife, Catherine, wave to the cheering crowds who filled the streets of London to celebrate their wedding on April 29, 2011.

Succession to the Crown

The order in which members of the royal family stand in line to the throne used to be decided by order of birth and by sex. Princes came ahead of princesses – so, had Elizabeth had a younger brother, he'd have become King. That changed in 2013, with a new law that put an end to the male preference.

Charitable work

Supporting charitable organizations is an important part of the work of the royal family. The Queen is patron to over 600 charities. Prince Charles founded the Prince's Trust, which gives help to young people in Britain and around the world. He also champions environmental issues and rural crafts. The Duke and Duchess of Cambridge and Prince Harry set up the Royal Foundation, working for the welfare of service personnel, young people and conservation projects.

Princes in uniform

Both William and Harry have followed family tradition by joining the armed forces.

Prince Harry served for just over two months with the British Army in Afghanistan.

William has trained to fly helicopters as a search and rescue pilot for the RAF.

The way of the Windsors

No monarch's reign has been straightforward, and the Windsors have faced many challenges. But, through world wars and personal and political crises, they have adapted the role of the royal family with the changing times.

The Duke and Duchess of Cambridge and Prince George greet well wishers at Princess Charlotte's christening, July 5, 2015.

Royal places of interest in the United Kingdom and Ireland

Key

- Royal residences
- Castles
- Coronation sites
- Battle sites

Castle of Mey

Battle of Culloden

Balmoral Castle

SCOTLAND

Scone

Stirling Castle

Dunfermline Palace

Iona Abbey

Edinburgh

Palace of Holyroodhouse

Dunadd

Edinburgh Castle

NORTHERN IRELAND

Belfast

Carrickfergus Castle

Bolton Castle

Lancaster

York

Battle of the Boyne

Beaumaris Castle

ENGLAND

Pontefract Castle

Hill of Tara

Dublin Castle

Dublin

Caernarfon Castle

Caernarfon

Chester

Sandringham House

IRELAND

Battle of Bosworth

Geddington

Battle of Naseby

Cromwell's House

Offa's Dyke

WALES

Worcester

Oxford

Christ Church

Sutton Hoo

Cardiff

You can find out more about the places shown on this map on pages 176-183.

A map of London and its royal sites of interest can be found on page 177.

Windsor Castle
Runnymede

London

Winchester

Battle of Hastings

Osborne House

Brighton Royal Pavilion

FACTFILE

Read on to find out more about Britain's
kings and queens. You'll find information
on places to visit, the Crown Jewels, royal
ceremonies and awards, and a glossary that
explains any difficult or unusual words.

ROYAL GOVERNMENT

Britain is a constitutional monarchy. This means that the country is governed by an elected Parliament alongside a monarch whose powers are largely symbolic.

This system is the result of a long tug-of-war, during which the balance of power has gradually shifted from the monarchy to Parliament.

The rise of Parliament

Anglo-Saxon and Norman kings had the final say in how to run their kingdoms. But no king could rule successfully without the support of his subjects, so most consulted a council of nobles before making laws, raising taxes or going to war.

In 1215, King John faced a rebellion by his nobles. They forced him to sign *Magna Carta*, an agreement protecting people's lives and property, and promising justice and no illegal taxes.

During the 13th century, the King's Council became known as 'Parliament', and non-nobles, or 'Commoners' were included for the first time. Medieval kings called Parliament when they wanted to raise extra taxes. By Tudor times, monarchs exercised their authority through the laws they passed in Parliament. But they were still very much in charge, and chose when it met.

Revolutions and change

In 1642, fighting between Charles I and Parliament sparked a civil war. The King was executed in 1649, and for the next ten years, Britain was a republic.

In 1660, the monarchy was restored, but further turmoil soon followed. In the Glorious Revolution of 1688, the Catholic James II was deposed by his Protestant daughter Mary and her husband William of Orange, at Parliament's invitation. They passed the 1689 Bill of Rights,

ensuring frequent Parliaments, free elections and freedom of speech in Parliament. It also decreed that future monarchs had to be Protestants.

Under the Hanoverians, the power of the monarchy gradually declined, as royal ministers and Parliament played a greater role. During the 19th and early 20th centuries, the right to vote was extended to all adult men and women.

Today's style of constitutional monarchy was more or less set during Victoria's reign, when the monarch was described as having three rights: to be consulted, to encourage and to warn.

The role of the monarch today

Although MPs now run the country, they still swear an oath of allegiance to the monarch, who plays an important formal role in many aspects of government. Here are some of them:

◆ When MPs want to bring in a new law, they put a 'Bill' to the vote. If it is approved in the House of Commons, and in the Lords, then the monarch gives it 'Royal Assent'. This turns the Bill into an 'Act', which means it can become law.

◆ The monarch opens Parliament every year after its summer break, and after general elections, with a ceremony known as the State Opening of Parliament (see page 171).

◆ Before a general election, the Prime Minister asks the monarch to dismiss Parliament.

◆ After a general election, the monarch invites the leader of the party that has won the most seats in the House of Commons to become Prime Minister and to form a new government.

◆ Members of the royal family aren't allowed to stand for Parliament, and while there is no law to stop them, they don't vote in elections either.

◆ Modern monarchs advise and support Prime Ministers at weekly meetings, but they don't tell them what to do.

Queen Elizabeth II delivers her speech in the House of
Lords during the State Opening of Parliament.

ROYAL CEREMONIES

The pomp of royal ceremonies and events in Britain is watched with fascination by many people around the world. These traditions have developed fixed sets of rules over the centuries.

Coronations

The coronation ceremony formally marks the beginning of a monarch's reign. It is one of the oldest royal traditions, which has elements that date back to Anglo-Saxon times.

Westminster Abbey has been a coronation venue since 1066. After entering the Abbey, the king or queen swears an oath, based on the one sworn by Edgar in 973. The monarch sits on the coronation chair, which was built for Edward I and contains the Stone of Destiny (see pages 182 and 183). Here, the monarch is presented with the regalia (see pages 172-173) and crowned by the Archbishops of Canterbury and York.

Trooping the Colour

This pageant has marked the sovereign's birthday since the 18th century. Troops parade past the monarch, carrying their divisional flags known as colours.

Army bands take part in Trooping the Colour.

State visits

When foreign Heads of State visit Britain, they are given a ceremonial welcome and hosted by the monarch. The highlight of the visit is a grand banquet for around 170 guests held in the ballroom at Buckingham Palace.

Changing the Guard

Guards wearing red tunics and bearskin caps are stationed outside Buckingham Palace to protect the monarch. The Changing the Guard ceremony takes place in the summer, when replacement guards arrive at the beginning of a new shift. A band plays music to accompany the changeover.

Garden parties

Garden parties are held at Buckingham Palace and at Holyroodhouse. Individuals who have contributed to the country are invited.

Royal Ascot

Queen Anne founded the racecourse at Ascot, where the royal family still goes to watch horse racing every June. The monarch and royal party process along the track and watch the races from the Royal Enclosure.

This manuscript detail shows the coronation of Henry III. He holds a sceptre in his hand, as the crown is placed upon his head.

Elizabeth II and the Dean of Westminster process past the Yeomen of the Guard, before distributing 'Maundy money' at the Royal Maundy Service in 1973.

Royal Maundy Service

The Royal Maundy Service takes place on the Thursday before Easter. Since the 13th century, the monarch has marked this day by distributing gifts to the poor. The king or queen also used to wash their feet, after a biblical tradition, but James II was the last monarch to do this.

These days, Queen Elizabeth II visits a British cathedral to hand out 'Maundy money', in red and white purses, to one male and one female pensioner for every year she has lived.

Swan Upping

Swan Upping is a count of mute swans belonging to the monarch carried out by boat crews on the Thames. Its origins date from the 12th century, when swans were a delicacy fit for a king. When cygnets are spotted, a cry of "all up!" is raised. Then, the boat crews stop to weigh and measure the young. Today, the crews are concerned with swan conservation, and not feeding the monarch.

State Opening of Parliament

The monarch calls a new Parliament every year and after a general election. This is marked by a ceremony known as the State Opening of Parliament. It involves several curious customs.

In the morning, the Yeomen of the Guard search the cellars, in remembrance of the Gunpowder Plot. Before the Opening, an MP is also held 'hostage' at Buckingham Palace, to guarantee the monarch's safe return from the Houses of Parliament.

The Sovereign cannot enter the House of Commons, so a messenger known as Black Rod is sent to summon the MPs. They show their independence from the monarch by slamming the door in Black Rod's face. He has to bang on the door three times to gain entry. Then, the MPs walk to the House of Lords, where the monarch reads a speech outlining the government's plans.

CROWN JEWELS

Crown Jewels are royal ceremonial objects, or *regalia*, used in coronation ceremonies, and worn on special occasions throughout their reigns.

The Scottish, Welsh and English Crown Jewels together show the power, wealth and heritage of the monarchy in Britain.

The Honours of Scotland

The Honours of Scotland are the oldest set of Crown Jewels in Britain. The crown, sceptre and sword that make up the Honours were first used together at the coronation of Mary, Queen of Scots in 1543, when she was just a baby.

The crown is made of Scottish gold and set with pearls. The sceptre and sword were gifts from two different popes in 1494 and 1507.

The Honours of Wales

This set of regalia was created for Edward VIII's investiture as Prince of Wales in 1911. A new coronet (a crown worn by a prince or peer) was made for Prince Charles's investiture in 1969. The Honours are made of Welsh gold from Gwynedd, and are decorated with Welsh dragons.

The English Crown Jewels

Edward the Confessor assembled the first set of English Crown Jewels in the late 11th century. For 600 years they survived theft, accidents and wars. Then, in 1649, Charles I was deposed by Oliver Cromwell, and most of the Crown Jewels were destroyed. But the monarchy was restored with Charles II, and replacements were made.

The Crown Jewels of the UK

The set, created for Charles II, continues to be used to this day, with new jewels that have been added over the centuries. They are now known as the Crown Jewels of the United Kingdom. Decorated with 23,578 gems, they are the most valuable collection of regalia in the world.

St. Edward's Crown

This solid-gold crown takes its name from the crown worn by Edward the Confessor. The most important Crown Jewel, it is only ever used to crown the monarch. But it's so heavy that Victoria and Edward VII asked to be crowned with the lighter Imperial State Crown instead.

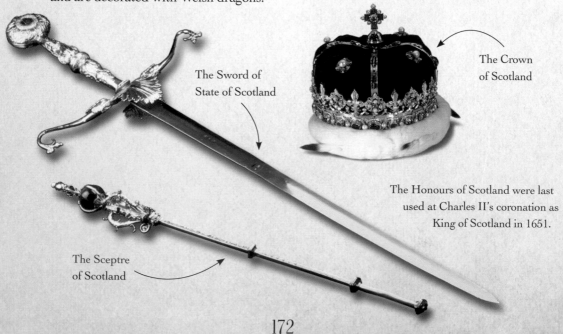

The Sword of State of Scotland

The Crown of Scotland

The Sceptre of Scotland

The Honours of Scotland were last used at Charles II's coronation as King of Scotland in 1651.

These are some of the Crown Jewels that are used in the coronation of British monarchs.

St. Edward's Crown

The Sovereign's Orb

The Sceptre with the Dove

The Sceptre with the Cross

The Imperial State Crown

The Imperial State Crown is worn by the monarch at the end of the coronation ceremony and at the State Opening of Parliament. It is set with 2,868 diamonds, 273 pearls, 17 sapphires, 11 emeralds and 5 rubies. These include the Stewart Sapphire from Charles II's crown, the Black Prince's ruby, two pearls that belonged to Elizabeth I, and a sapphire worn by Edward the Confessor when he was crowned.

Queen consorts' crowns

The wives of Edward VII, George V and George VI wore crowns set with the Koh-i-Noor diamond. Its name means 'mountain of light' in Persian. This diamond is said to bring good luck to women, but bad luck to men.

The Coronation Ring

The Coronation Ring symbolizes a monarch's 'marriage' to the nation. The present one was created for William IV.

The Sceptres

When a new monarch is crowned, he or she holds two staffs: the Sceptre with the Cross and the Sceptre with the Dove. The Sceptre with the Cross is set with the largest piece cut from the Cullinan diamond. The government of the Transvaal (now part of South Africa) gave the diamond to Edward VII in 1907.

The Sovereign's Orb

The Orb is also handed to the monarch as part of the coronation service. It is a hollow sphere made of gold and decorated with bands of gems. The Orb is topped with a cross.

Anointing spoon and ampulla

The 12th-century anointing spoon is the oldest piece of regalia. During the most sacred part of the coronation ceremony, the spoon is used to anoint the monarch with holy oil (see page 17). The oil is stored in an eagle-shaped flask known as an ampulla.

ROYAL AWARDS

The monarch gives awards to people at services called investitures. The idea behind this goes back over a thousand years, to when kings or queens wanted to reward the loyalty of their supporters.

Originally monarchs gave money or land, but later they gave titles and badges instead. For centuries only the wealthiest men received these. But kings and queens have made various awards available to all men, women, soldiers, civilians and even businesses.

Knighthoods

A knighthood is the highest title that a monarch can give to a person. The first knighthoods were granted to men who had served the monarch in battle. Over time, the title became symbolic, and was extended to men and women who had made any great contribution to the country.

Elizabeth I dubs a knight.

At a knight's investiture, the monarch places a sword on the left and then right shoulder of the kneeling recipient. This is called dubbing. Male knights are titled 'Sir' and female knights 'Dame'.

The Order of the Garter

Founded by Edward III in 1348, this is the oldest and most prestigious order of knighthood. Today, the Queen and some members of the royal family belong to the order, in addition to 24 chosen knights.

The Order's George badge depicts its patron saint, St. George, surrounded by a garter. On the garter are the words, *honi soit qui mal y pense*, which is old French for, 'shame on him who thinks this evil'. Its members meet at Windsor every June, where they process, wearing rich velvet robes and black velvet hats.

A Garter badge

This is a 16th-century engraving of a Garter procession at Windsor.

The Order of the Thistle

This Scottish order of knighthood is the second most important in Britain. It was officially created by James II in 1687 to reward Scottish nobles who had shown him support.

Queen Elizabeth II opened the order's membership up to women. Its motto is *nemo me impune lacessit*, which is Latin for, 'nobody harms me and gets away with it'.

Order of the British Empire

George V set up the OBE in 1917 as a reward for the efforts of men and women, in Britain and across the Empire, during the First World War.

Since its creation, the order has also been given to individuals who have contributed to the United Kingdom's success in various fields, such as the arts and sports. Today, government bodies decide who should receive the award, but the monarch still presents it, at a special ceremony in Buckingham Palace.

There are several levels within the order. The first is Member (MBE), then Officer (OBE), next Commander (CBE), then Knight/Dame (K/DBE), and lastly, the most important, Knight Grand Cross/Dame Grand Cross (GBE).

The Victoria Cross

Queen Victoria was so impressed by the bravery of soldiers from Britain and across the Empire in the Crimean War that she created a new medal, the Victoria Cross, or VC. The Queen insisted that any deserving soldier, from any background and of any military rank, should be entitled to it.

Most VCs have been made from the metal of two cannons captured in the Crimean War.

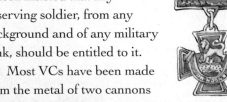
A Victoria Cross

The George Cross

Only soldiers who have fought in direct contact with the enemy can receive the VC. But, during the Second World War, George VI wanted to reward soldiers and civilians who performed acts of courage away from the front line. So he established the George Cross, or GC, in 1940. Together with the VC, it remains the highest award for bravery.

A George Cross

The Queen's Gallantry Medal

Queen Elizabeth II created the Queen's Gallantry Medal in 1974. The award recognizes individuals who have demonstrated great bravery in peacetime.

The Royal Medal

The Royal Medal was introduced by George IV to reward scientific achievements. Since then, silver-gilt medals bearing a portrait of the reigning king or queen have been presented to eminent scientists by the monarch every year.

Royal Warrants

Kings and queens have always shown their preference for particular manufacturers. By the 15th century, it had become customary for the monarch to give a Royal Warrant of Appointment to an individual or company that provided the royal family with a specific product.

Three centuries later, businesses holding a Royal Warrant began displaying the arms of the monarch at their shops. Today, companies supplying the monarch with any product, from light bulbs to baked beans, can show the royal arms on their packaging.

PLACES TO VISIT

There are historic royal sites to visit all across the British Isles, from castles and palaces, to battlefields and coronation sites. Here are some of the most important ones. For more information, visit the Usborne Quicklinks Website at www.usborne-quicklinks.com

LONDON

Buckingham Palace

This palace has been the British monarch's home in London since Queen Victoria's time. Visitors today can view the Changing the Guard through the gates, tour the State Rooms and see art and objects from the Royal Collection.

Tower of London

William the Conqueror first built the Tower after his victory at Hastings in 1066. In its 900-year history, the Tower has been used as a royal fortress, a palace, a prison and even a zoo. In Tudor times, Anne Boleyn, Catherine Howard and Lady Jane Grey were all beheaded here.

Today, seven ravens are kept at the Tower and looked after by an official known as the Raven Master. There is a superstition that if the ravens ever leave, the Tower will fall down.

The world-famous Crown Jewels can be seen in the Jewel House. They are guarded by the Yeomen Warders – better known as the 'Beefeaters'.

A polar bear and an elephant were once kept at the Tower.

St. James's Palace

Henry VIII built this red-brick palace, where Mary Tudor signed the treaty surrendering Calais and Elizabeth I lived at the time of the Spanish Armada. It's still officially the primary royal residence, although since the reign of Queen Victoria, all monarchs have lived at Buckingham Palace instead.

Westminster

Edward the Confessor founded an abbey and a royal palace at Westminster. All that remains of the palace is Westminster Hall, which was erected during William II's reign.

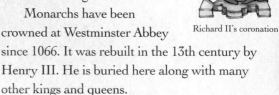

Richard II's coronation

Monarchs have been crowned at Westminster Abbey since 1066. It was rebuilt in the 13th century by Henry III. He is buried here along with many other kings and queens.

The Banqueting House

This building is all that's left of the Palace of Whitehall, which was home to kings and queens in the 16th and 17th centuries, until it was destroyed by a fire in 1698.

The Banqueting House was built for James I as a venue for theatrical parties, or masques. However, it's best known as the site of his son Charles I's execution in 1649.

Clarence House

Today, Prince Charles shares Clarence House with his wife and sons, as their official London residence. It was built for William IV, but became famous as Queen Elizabeth the Queen Mother's home. The house is open to visitors in the summer.

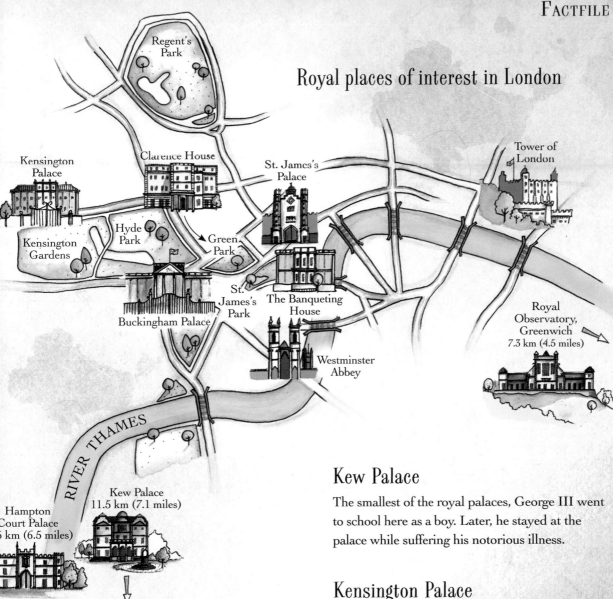

Royal places of interest in London

Regent's Park

Kensington Palace

Clarence House

St. James's Palace

Tower of London

Hyde Park

Green Park

Kensington Gardens

St. James's Park

The Banqueting House

Royal Observatory, Greenwich
7.3 km (4.5 miles)

Buckingham Palace

Westminster Abbey

RIVER THAMES

Kew Palace
11.5 km (7.1 miles)

Hampton Court Palace
5 km (6.5 miles)

Kew Palace

The smallest of the royal palaces, George III went to school here as a boy. Later, he stayed at the palace while suffering his notorious illness.

Kensington Palace

William and Mary founded Kensington as a royal palace away from the smelly river. It was the birthplace of Queen Victoria, and more recently, home to Diana, Princess of Wales.

Hampton Court Palace

This palace was built for Henry VIII's Lord Chancellor, Cardinal Wolsey, but became a home for Tudor and Stuart monarchs. Henry VIII added tennis courts, bowling alleys and a lavatory, which 28 people could use at the same time.

You can see the Great Hall, where Shakespeare's actors performed for James I, and get lost in its famous maze. Visitors should watch out for the ghost of Henry VIII's fifth wife, Catherine Howard, in the so-called Haunted Gallery.

Greenwich

Monarchs used to stay at Greenwich in the 16th and 17th centuries. The Tudor palace, where Henry VIII was born, no longer stands. But you can still visit the grand Queen's House, home to the wives of James I and Charles I, and the Royal Observatory, founded by Charles II in 1675.

England

Runnymede, Berkshire

Alfred the Great's council of nobles used to meet in the water-meadow at Runnymede. It was here, in 1215, that King John was forced to sign *Magna Carta*.

King John signs *Magna Carta*.

Windsor Castle, Berkshire

Windsor is the largest and oldest castle in the world that is still a home. It was originally built by William the Conqueror. His wooden castle stood on the site of today's Round Tower.

In 1992, a fire swept through the castle damaging and destroying over 100 rooms. Since then, it has been restored to a new level of grandeur. Queen Mary's dolls' house, the most famous royal toy, is on display in the castle.

Ten kings and queens are buried here in St. George's Chapel, where you can also see the banners of the Order of the Garter's members.

Frogmore House, Berkshire

Frogmore House was the much-loved home of Queen Victoria. She found its grounds so peaceful that she had the Royal Mausoleum built there as a burial place for her and Prince Albert.

Frogmore is open to the public one weekend in August each year. Visitors can see the pictures painted by Queen Victoria and her children that decorate the house.

Royal Pavilion in Brighton

Royal Pavilion, Brighton

George IV's Royal Pavilion is unlike any other royal residence ever built in the UK. The extravagant king created the building according to a fantastic oriental design, as a venue for his lavish banquets and musical parties.

This is a view of Windsor Castle taken from the Long Walk, a processional route first laid out by Charles II. The Round Tower stands on the far left.

Cromwell's House, Cambridgeshire

Oliver Cromwell's home in Ely, Cambridgeshire, has been recreated to show how he and his family lived during the English Civil War.

Hatfield House, Hertfordshire

Hatfield House was built by Elizabeth I's Chief Minister, Robert Cecil. The Queen herself spent much of her childhood in the Old Palace that stands nearby, in the house's park. You can find the oak tree where the young Elizabeth first learned that she was Queen.

Osborne House, Isle of Wight

Queen Victoria and her family used to spend their summer holidays here. Her husband, Prince Albert, helped to design the building and grounds himself, including a Swiss chalet, where the royal children played. Victoria died in her bedroom at Osborne in 1901.

Hever Castle, Kent

This castle was home to the young Anne Boleyn, before her fateful marriage to Henry VIII.

Leeds Castle, Kent

Medieval English kings from Edward I to Henry V gave this castle to their wives. Its final royal resident, Henry VIII, used to visit the castle with his first wife, Catherine of Aragon. He also stayed here on his way to the Field of the Cloth of Gold, in France, in 1520.

Bosworth, Leicestershire

Rose of York

Tudor Rose

Rose of Lancaster

In 1485, Henry VII defeated Richard III on the battlefield at Bosworth, bringing the Wars of the Roses to an end. You can find out how he did it at the museum near the battlefield site.

Sandringham House, Norfolk

Sandringham has been the monarch's country retreat for four generations. Elizabeth II first opened the estate to the public, as part of her Silver Jubilee celebrations. Since then, visitors have been able to explore the house and parkland where the royal family spends Christmas.

Eleanor Cross at Geddington, Northamptonshire

In 1290, Edward I marked the route his wife Eleanor of Castile's coffin took from Lincoln, where she died, to Westminster Abbey, by putting up 12 stone crosses along the way.

Over 700 years later, only three original crosses remain, at Waltham Cross, Northampton and Geddington, while a replica one stands at Charing Cross in London.

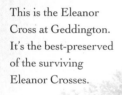

This is the Eleanor Cross at Geddington. It's the best-preserved of the surviving Eleanor Crosses.

Naseby, Northamptonshire

A monument marks the site of the battlefield where Charles I was defeated by Cromwell and the Parliamentarian army in 1645.

Parliamentarian troops

Allerton Castle, North Yorkshire

George III's son, Prince Frederick, used to live at Allerton Castle. He is better known as the 'Grand Old Duke of York' in the famous nursery rhyme:

"The Grand Old Duke of York,
  He had ten thousand men;
  He marched them up to the top of the hill,
  And he marched them down again..."

These lines are said to have been inspired by his workmen marching up and down Allerton Hill, while building a summerhouse known as the Temple of Victory for him. Today, you can march up the hill to visit the summerhouse, and march back down again.

Bolton Castle, North Yorkshire

Following her abdication, Mary, Queen of Scots was held prisoner in Bolton Castle for a year in 1568. Today, you can explore the castle and the surrounding Yorkshire Dales, where Mary is believed to have walked and gone hunting.

Christ Church, Oxford

This Oxford college was founded by Cardinal Wolsey as Cardinal's College in 1524. Five years later, Wolsey fell from power, and Henry VIII renamed the college Christ Church.

During the English Civil War, Charles I moved to Oxford. He lived in the college, worshipped in its cathedral and held a parliament in its Great Hall.

Sutton Hoo, Suffolk

The grave of an Anglo-Saxon king, where his most-prized possessions were buried in a ship, was discovered here in 1939. The burial chamber has been recreated for visitors to see. Original and replica royal treasures, including weapons and drinking horns, are on display.

Drinking horns

Battle Abbey, Sussex

The abbey built by William the Conqueror, to commemorate the Battle of Hastings and those who died fighting, is now in ruins. Visitors can tour the abbey's remains and the acres of battlefield. A plaque even marks the site where King Harold is thought to have been killed.

King Harold

Pontefract Castle, West Yorkshire

Richard II met a sticky end here in 1400. Later, during the English Civil War, it became a Royalist stronghold, and was repeatedly attacked by the Parliamentarians. The attacks reduced it to a ruin, but visitors can see the cellars where weapons were stored at the time.

WALES

Caernarfon Castle, Gwynedd

Edward I built this impressive castle to mark his conquest of Wales. His son, the first English Prince of Wales, was born here in 1284. Prince Charles was crowned here, as Prince of Wales, in 1969. Today visitors can take a walk along its towering walls.

Beaumaris Castle, Gwynedd

Beaumaris was the last castle built by Edward I, as part of his successful campaign to bring the whole of Wales under English rule. It's notable for its almost perfectly symmetrical shape, and is recognized as a World Heritage Site.

Offa's Dyke, Powys

King Offa built this defensive earthwork in the late 8th century, to separate the Anglo-Saxon kingdom of Mercia from the Welsh kingdom of Powys. There is an exhibition here to explain how and why, and a National Trail path, which follows the course and remains of this great earthwork.

SCOTLAND

Balmoral Castle, Aberdeenshire

Queen Victoria thought of Balmoral as her "dear paradise in the Highlands". It remains the best-loved home of the royal family in Scotland.

Dunadd, Argyll and Bute

The remains of a hill fort still poke through the grass at Dunadd, the capital of the ancient Scottish kingdom of Dalriada. At the top of the hill, there is a slab carved with a footprint, which the first rulers of Scotland would step into during king-making ceremonies.

The Castle of Mey, Caithness

George VI's widow, the Queen Mother bought this castle in 1952 and restored it as a holiday home, where she spent almost 50 summers. Only minor alterations have been made since she died in 2002, so visitors can see the castle as it was in her lifetime.

Edinburgh Castle, Edinburgh

Situated on top of an extinct volcano, this castle is closely linked with Scotland's royal history. David I built the first royal castle here in the 12th century. Its original chapel still stands despite the bombardment the castle suffered during the Scottish Wars of Independence, the Civil War, the Glorious Revolution and the Jacobite uprisings.

Today, you can find the Scottish Crown Jewels, known as the Honours of Scotland, on show in the Crown Room. They are displayed alongside the Stone of Destiny – the coronation stone used by early Scottish kings and still used by modern British monarchs.

Honours of Scotland

Palace of Holyroodhouse, Edinburgh

This is the monarch's official residence in Scotland, where royal events and ceremonies are staged. Holyroodhouse was originally built for Scottish kings in the 15th century, and between 1561 and 1567 Mary, Queen of Scots lived and got married here. Portraits of both real and legendary Scottish kings can be seen in the Great Gallery.

Royal Yacht *Britannia*, Edinburgh

For centuries, the British monarch has had a purpose-built royal yacht to travel the seas.

Queen Elizabeth II's yacht was called *Britannia*. She made visits to many countries on board, while her children used it for their honeymoons. *Britannia* was retired in 1997, and moored in Leith, near Edinburgh, for the public to see inside its cabins.

Dunfermline Palace, Fife

Many Scottish kings and queens have lived here since the 11th century. It was last used by Charles II during the Civil War, but its ruined walls still stand. The grave of Robert the Bruce can be visited at the nearby Dunfermline Abbey.

Dumbarton Rock, Glasgow

From the 5th century until 1018, the capital of the British kingdom of Strathclyde was based on Dumbarton Rock. A castle that served as a refuge for Scottish royalty was later built on the site.

This is a Victorian illustration of the Palace of Holyroodhouse in Edinburgh. The Palace looks the same today, but the new Scottish Parliament building now stands to the front of it.

Iona Abbey, Iona

A 9th-century Celtic cross

Between the 9th and the 11th centuries, early Scottish kings, including MacBeth, were buried in the Abbey's cemetery.

Scone, Perthshire

Scottish kings were crowned at Scone, upon the Stone of Destiny, from the time of Kenneth MacAlpin. The stone is now held at Edinburgh Castle, but a replica can be seen marking the original coronation site.

Stirling Castle, Stirlingshire

Visitors to Stirling Castle can see its Great Hall where the baptism of James VI of Scotland (later James I of England) was celebrated with three days of festivities. The battles of Stirling Bridge and Bannockburn were fought in the land surrounding the castle.

Linlithgow Palace, West Lothian

Linlithgow Palace is now in ruins, but it was once the grand home of Scottish kings and queens. Mary, Queen of Scots was born here in 1542.

A fountain is said to have flowed with wine here, to celebrate Bonnie Prince Charlie's arrival in 1745. You can now see the fountain that has been restored and placed in the palace courtyard.

NORTHERN IRELAND

Carrickfergus Castle, County Antrim

King John captured this castle in 1210, to use as an English base in Ireland. William of Orange arrived here before the Battle of the Boyne, where he finally defeated James II.

IRELAND

Dublin Castle, Dublin

Dublin Castle was the English monarchy's main base in Ireland for 700 years. The Irish Crown Jewels were stolen from the castle in 1907 and have never been recovered.

Battle of the Boyne, County Louth

There is an exhibition at the site of the famous battle between the Catholic James II and the Protestant William of Orange.

James II's troops

Hill of Tara, County Meath

This archaeological site is associated with the High Kings of Ireland. The remains of tombs, forts and standing stones can still be seen today.

GLOSSARY

This glossary explains some of the words you may come across when reading this book. If a word used in the glossary has an entry of its own, it is shown in *italic* type.

abbot The head of a *monastery*.

abdicate To give up the *throne*.

Act The result of a decision made by a *parliament*.

allegiance Loyal support for someone or some cause.

allies People who fight on the same side in a war.

anoint To bless with holy oil.

archbishop A senior priest, in charge of the Church over a large area. Priests in the rank below this are called bishops.

assassinate To murder a leader or politician.

Bill A decision that is to be discussed in a *parliament*.

Britannia An ancient name for Britain in *Latin*.

burgh A Scottish name for a town where people first gathered to buy and sell goods.

burh An Anglo-Saxon name for a fortified town.

Catholicism A branch of the Christian Church which is led by the *Pope*.

Celtic 1. The languages spoken by the pre-Roman inhabitants of Britain. 2. Anything relating to Celtic-speaking people and their culture.

civil war A war in which armies from the same country fight each other.

civilian Anyone who is not a member of the armed forces.

colony A country, or region, that has been settled in and is ruled by people from another country.

Commonwealth 1. The *government* led by Oliver Cromwell after the execution of Charles I at the end of the English *Civil War*. 2. The association of countries which were formerly members of the British *Empire*.

consort The husband or wife of a *monarch*.

conspirator A person making a secret illegal plan.

constitution A set of laws used to rule a group or country.

constitutional monarchy A form of *government* in which a *monarch* is the *Head of State*, but a *parliament* holds political power.

coronation A ceremony in which a new *monarch* is crowned.

coronet A smaller crown worn by a *prince* or a *peer*.

court A name for both the residence and the *courtiers* of a *monarch*.

courtier A *monarch's* attendant.

Crown Jewels the crowns, jewels and *regalia* worn by a *monarch* on state occasions.

democracy A political system in which citizens can freely *elect* people to represent them in *government*.

depose To remove someone from a position of power.

divine right of kings The belief that *monarchs* are chosen by God, and that only God can judge their actions.

dynasty A series of rulers from the same family.

empire A group of countries or territories under the control of another country.

execute To kill a person who has been sentenced to death by law.

exile To be sent away from your country and ordered not to return.

faction A group of people, united by their shared views.

figurehead A person who has an important position but no real powers.

fleet A group of ships.

fortress A group of buildings surrounded by a wall so that they can be easily defended.

general A soldier who leads an army.

general election An election to choose the ruling political party in some countries.

government The group of people who run a country.

Head of State A country's top public representative.

heir The person who will inherit, by law, the property or titles of someone when they die.

hill fort A fortified hilltop settlement.

homage A public show of respect to someone.

invade To enter an area intending to take control of it.

investiture The ceremony at which a person receives a title or *regalia*.

Jacobite A supporter of James Stuart, Queen Anne's *Catholic* half brother, or his son, Charles (Bonnie Prince Charlie).

jubilee A celebration to mark an anniversary.

king A male, royal ruler of a country.

kingdom An area that is ruled by a *king* or *queen*.

knight 1. A man in the Middle Ages who was trained to fight on horseback. 2. A title given by the *monarch* to reward people for their services and achievements.

Latin The language spoken by the people of ancient Rome and the Roman empire. It was also used by scholars in *medieval* Europe.

manuscript A handwritten document.

marches Bordering areas between England, Scotland and Wales.

medieval Anything relating to the Middle Ages.

minister 1. Someone high up in *government*. 2. A clergyman.

minority 1. A small number or part within a larger group. 2. The period when a person is below legal age.

monarch A *king* or *queen*.

monarchy A system of *government* in which a country is ruled by a *monarch*.

monastery A group of buildings where *monks* live and work.

monk A man who lives in a *monastery* and has devoted his life to God.

noble A member of a family that belongs to the ruling class, or nobility, of a country.

occupy To seize and take control of an area.

overlord A *king* who claims authority over lesser *kings*.

overthrow To defeat and remove a leader from power.

pagan A person who doesn't believe in a single God.

parliament A group of people who meet to make decisions and create laws for their country.

parliamentarian A supporter of *parliament*.

partition The division of a country into two or more separate nations.

peasant A person of low status in the Middle Ages, who works on the land.

peer A male *noble* holding the title of baron, viscount, earl, marquess or duke (in increasing order of significance) or a female holding the title baroness, countess or duchess in her own right.

petition A written document signed by a number of people, requesting some form of action from a *government* or other authority.

Pope The head of the *Catholic* Church, who resides in Rome.

Presbyterians *Protestants* with similar beliefs to *Puritans*.

Prime Minister The leader of a *government* in some countries.

prince 1. A son of a *monarch*, or of a prince. 2. A ruler of a *principality*.

princess A daughter of a *monarch*, or of a *prince*.

principality A *territory* ruled by a *prince*.

Protestant Reformation An attempt in the 16th century to reform the *Catholic* Church, which resulted in *Protestantism*.

Protestantism A branch of the Christian Church that does not have the *Pope* as its leader.

Puritans Strict *Protestants* who believe in a simple life.

queen 1. A female *monarch*. 2. The wife of a *king*.

rebellion An organized resistance to a *government* or other authority by rebels.

regalia The ceremonial symbols and decorations of *royalty*.

regent A person who rules a country in the absence of a *monarch*.

reign To rule as *king* or *queen*.

republic A country without a *king* or *queen*, ruled by leaders on behalf of the people.

Restoration The re-establishment of the *monarchy* in 1660, with the *reign* of Charles II.

revolt A *rebellion* against authority.

revolution The overthrowing of a leader or *government* by the people.

royalist A supporter of the *monarchy*.

royalty The *king* or *queen* and his or her family.

settlement A collection of buildings and people making a community.

skirmish A short battle or fight between armies.

Sovereign A *king* or *queen*.

state An area with its own laws. A state can be independent, or part of a larger country.

subject A person who lives under the rule of a monarch.

succession The act of coming after another person.

taxes Money collected from the people by a *government* or a ruler.

territory An area of land ruled by a particular group or *government*.

terrorist A person who uses violence for political purposes.

throne 1. A chair for a *king*, *queen* or bishop. 2. A symbol of *monarchy*.

treason An act seen as a betrayal of a country or leader, such as trying to overthrow a *government*.

treaty An agreement between people or countries.

tribe A group of people who share common ancestry, cultural, religious and regional origins.

uprising A *rebellion* or *revolt*.

warlord A local ruler who controls an army.

Reigns of the Kings and Queens

ANGLO-SAXONS & VIKINGS
Alfred the Great (871-899)
Edward the Elder (899-924)
Aelfweard (924)
Athelstan (924-939)
Edmund I (939-946)
Edred (946-955)
Edwig (955-959)
Edgar the Peaceful (959-975)
Edward II the Martyr (975-978)
Ethelred the Unready (978-1013, 1014-1016)
Swein (1013-1014)
Edmund Ironside (1016)
Cnut (1016-1035)
Harthacnut (1035-42)
Harold I Harefoot (1037-1040)
Edward the Confessor (1042-66)
Harold II (1066)

THE NORMANS
William I (1066-1087)
William II (1087-1100)
Henry I (1100-1135)
Stephen (1135-1154)
Matilda (1141)

THE PLANTAGENETS
Henry II (1154-1189)
Richard I (1189-1199)
John (1199-1216)
Henry III (1216-1272)
Edward I (1272-1307)
Edward II (1307-1327)
Edward III (1327-1377)
Richard II (1377-1399)
Henry IV (1399-1413)
Henry V (1413-1422)
Henry VI (1422-61, 1470-71)
Edward IV (1461-70, 1471-83)
Edward V (1483)
Richard III (1483-1485)

THE TUDORS
Henry VII (1485-1509)
Henry VIII (1509-1547)
Edward VI (1547-1553)
Lady Jane Grey (1553)
Mary I (1553-1558)
Elizabeth I (1558-1603)

EARLY SCOTTISH KINGS
Kenneth I MacAlpin (c. 839-858)
Donald I (858-862)
Constantine I (862-876)
Aedh (876-878)
Giric (878-889)
Eocha (878-889)
Donald II (889-900)
Constantine II (900-943)
Malcolm I (943-954)
Indulf (954-962)
Duff (962-966)
Culen (966-971)
Kenneth II (971-995)
Constantine III (995-997)
Kenneth III (997-1005)
Malcolm II (1005-1034)

THE DUNKELDS
Duncan I (1034-1040)
MacBeth (1040-1057)
Lulach (1057-1058)
Malcolm III (1058-1093)
Donald III (1093-94, 1094-97)
Duncan II (1094)
Edgar (1097-1107)
Alexander I (1107-1124)
David I (1124-1153)
Malcolm IV (1153-1165)
William I (1165-1214)
Alexander II (1214-1249)
Alexander III (1249-1286)
Margaret (1286-1290)

THE BALLIOLS
John Balliol (1292-1296)
Edward Balliol (1332-1356)

THE BRUCES
Robert I (1306-1329)
David II (1329-1371)

THE STEWARTS
Robert II (1371-1390)
Robert III (1390-1406)
James I (1406-1437)
James II (1437-1460)
James III (1460-1488)
James IV (1488-1513)
James V (1513-1542)
Mary, Queen of Scots (1542-67)

THE STUARTS
James VI & I (1567 & 1603-25)
Charles I (1625-1649)
Charles II (1660-1685)
James II (1685-1688)
William III (1689-1702) &
Mary II (1689-1694)
Anne (1702-1714)

THE HANOVERIANS
George I (1714-1727)
George II (1727-1760)
George III (1760-1820)
George IV (1820-1830)
William IV (1830-1837)
Victoria (1837-1901)

SAXE-COBURG-GOTHA
Edward VII (1901-1910)

THE WINDSORS
George V (1910-1936)
Edward VIII (1936)
George VI (1936-1952)
Elizabeth II (1952-present)

You can read about some of the early Welsh Kings and High Kings of Ireland on pages 18-19 and 24-25.

INDEX OF BRITISH MONARCHS

INDEX

ACKNOWLEDGEMENTS

Every effort has been made to trace and acknowledge ownership of copyright. If any rights have been omitted, the publishers offer to rectify this in any future editions following notification. The publishers are grateful to the following individuals and organizations for their permission to reproduce material on the following pages:

Cover: Queen Elizabeth I - The Pelican Portrait by Nicholas Hilliard © Walker Art Gallery, National Museums Liverpool/Bridgeman Images; p1 © National Library of Scotland, Edinburgh, Scotland/Bridgeman Art Library; p2-3 © Society of Antiquaries of London, UK/The Bridgeman Art Library; p4-5 © Victoria & Albert Museum, London, UK/The Bridgeman Art Library; p6 © British Library Board. All Rights Reserved/The Bridgeman Art Library; p10 © MasterBliss/Alamy; p11 © The British Library Board. All rights reserved, Add. 10292 f.164; p12 © The Granger Collection/TopFoto; p14 © Detail Heritage/Alamy; p15 © Ashmolean Museum, University of Oxford/The Bridgeman Art Library; p18 © Homer Sykes/CORBIS; p19 By permission of LlyfrgellCymru/The National Library of Wales; p20 © National Museums of Scotland/The Bridgeman Art Library; p21 © Duncan Shaw/Alamy; p22 © David Cairns/Alamy; p24 © Destinations/Corbis; p26 © Bymuseum, Oslo, Norway/Index/The Bridgeman Art Library; p29 With special authorisation of the city of Bayeux/The Bridgeman Art Library; p30-31 © David Rowland/Alamy; p34-35 © Musée de la Tapisserie, Bayeux/The Bridgeman Art Library; p35 © Museum of London, UK/The Bridgeman Art Library; p36 © Eye35.com/Alamy; p37 © Topham Picturepoint/topfoto.co.uk; p39 (top) © Alexei Fateev/Alamy; p39 (bottom) © David Ball/Alamy; p40 © British Library Board, All Rights Reserved/The Bridgeman Art Library; p41 © The Art Archive/British Library; p42 © Private Collection/The Bridgeman Art Library; p43(top) © National Museums Scotland. Licensor www.scran.ac.uk; p43 © Malcolm Fifc/Alamy; p44 © British Library Board, All Rights Reserved/The Bridgeman Art Library; p45 © British Library, London/Bridgeman Art Library; p48-49 © The Art Archive/Alamy; p50 © Tremorvpix/Alamy; p51 © British Library Board, All Rights Reserved/The Bridgeman Art Library; p53 The Master and Fellows of Corpus Christi College, Cambridge; p54 © Angelo Hornak/Alamy; p55 © British Library Board, All Rights Reserved/The Bridgeman Art Library; p56 © British Library Board, All Rights Reserved/The Bridgeman Art Library; p57 © Paul Vidler/Alamy; p58 © The British Library/HIP/Topfoto; p59 © John McKenna/Alamy; p60 © John McKenna/Alamy; p62 © Angelo Hornak/Alamy; p63 © Collection of the Earl of Leicester, Holkham Hall, Norfolk/The Bridgeman Art Library; p64 © Private Collection/The Bridgeman Art Library; p65 © Bibliothèque Nationale, Paris/The Bridgeman Art Library; p66 © The British Library/HIP/Topfoto; p68 © Westminster Abbey, London/The Bridgeman Art Library; p72 © Philip Mould Collection, London/the Bridgeman Art Library; p73 © David Angel/Alamy; p75 © Scottish National Portrait Gallery, Edinburgh, Scotland/The Bridgeman Art Library; p76 © The Art Archive/Alamy; p77 © National Portrait Gallery, London/The Bridgeman Art Library; p78 © Robert Harding Picture Library Ltd/Alamy; p80 © Private Collection/The Bridgeman Art Library; p81 © Lambeth Palace Library, London/The Bridgeman Art Library; p82 © Wuerttembergische Landesbibliothek, Stuttgart, Cod. hist. 4° 141, p. 97.; p83 © Scottish Viewpoint/Alamy; p84 © Private Collection/The Bridgeman Art Library; p85 © Royal Holloway, University of London/The Bridgeman Art Library; p88 Private Collection/Photo © Christie's Images/The Bridgeman Art Library; p90 © Scottish National Portrait Gallery, Edinburgh, Scotland/The Bridgeman Art Library; p91 © Private Collection/The Bridgeman Art Library; p92 © Belvoir Castle, Leicestershire, UK/The Bridgeman Art Library; p93 © Chateau de Versailles, France/Giraudon/The Bridgeman Art Library; p94 © Graham Harrison/Alamy; p95 © Hever Castle, Kent, UK/The Bridgeman Art Library; p96 © Louvre, Paris, France/Giraudon/The Bridgeman Art Library; p96-97 © Tony French/Alamy; p98 © Falkland Palace, Falkland, Fife, Scotland/Mark Fiennes/The Bridgeman Art Library; p100 © National Gallery of Art, Washington DC, USA/The Bridgeman Art Library; p101 © National Gallery, London, UK/The Bridgeman Art Library; p102 © Society of Antiquaries of London, UK/The Bridgeman Art Library; p103 © Bruce Ashford/Alamy; p105 (top left) © The Gallery Collection/

Picture research by Ruth King & Samantha Noonan
Digital design by John Russell
Additional design by Brenda Cole

This edition first published in 2016 by Usborne Publishing Ltd., Usborne House, 83–85 Saffron Hill, London, EC1N 8RT, United Kingdom. www.usborne.com Copyright © 2016, 2012, 2010 Usborne Publishing Ltd. The name Usborne and the devices ♀⊕ are Trade Marks of Usborne Publishing Ltd. All rights reserved. No part of this publication may be reproduced, stored in any retrieval system, or transmitted in any form or by any means, electronic, mechanical, photocopying, recording or otherwise, without the prior permission of the publisher. Printed in China. UE